DESCENDANTS

OF

SAMUEL SPARE.

COMPILED BY

JOHN SPARE, A. M., M. D.

ORDERED TO BE PRINTED BY

*JOHN C. SPARE,   ABBY C. MEAD,   GEORGE E. SPARE,
SAMUEL SPARE,   JOHN V. SPARE,   JOHN SPARE,
CHARLES E. BELCHER and ADELAIDE L BELCHER.*

NEW BEDFORD, MASS.:
PAUL HOWLAND, JR., PRINTER AND ENGRAVER.
1884.

In the interest of creating a more extensive selection of rare historical book reprints, we have chosen to reproduce this title even though it may possibly have occasional imperfections such as missing and blurred pages, missing text, poor pictures, markings, dark backgrounds and other reproduction issues beyond our control. Because this work is culturally important, we have made it available as a part of our commitment to protecting, preserving and promoting the world's literature. Thank you for your understanding.

LAMB TAVERN.—Stood on the site of the present Adams House, on Washington Street.

DESCENDANTS OF SAMUEL SPARE.

PART I.—NAMES IN THE MALE LINE.

NOTES.—b. for born; d., died; m., married; bef., before; ab., about; r, residence; ch., church or children; bap., baptized; l., living.

The bold figures refer to a succeeding page. The bold letters to Part II.

SAMUEL SPARE was b. doubtless in England, between July 5, 1683, and July 5, 1684; d. in Canton, July 5, 1768. m. Elizabeth ———, of London; b. ab. 1694; d., Canton, Oct. 10, 1774. Children:

 i. or ii. SAMUEL², b. ———; "burial," Boston, Sept. 27, 1734, doubtless on Copp's Hill
 ii. or i. Child; died on the passage over.
 iii. "Daughter," bap. May y⁰ 6, 1733; name left blank on ch. records; probably d. young in Canton.
1 iv. JOHN², b., Boston, Oct. 17, 1737; bap., Oct. 23; d., June 6, 1820

FIRST ARRIVAL.—In what year Samuel Spare, with wife and two children, sailed from England, and arrived in this country, has not been ascertained. The first date confirming his presence in Boston is 1729. This is merely incidental; it is found on Christ Church records, wherein it is recorded, "Baptized Margerett, Negro slave of Samuel Spear, July y⁰ 5, 1729." The early records of the church contain only "Baptisms," "Marriages," and "Burials," so that if the first of any of these, that affected this family, occurred at this date, Samuel Spare may have been a few years earlier in Boston. Against its being more than a few, we have the evidence that his wife was born about 1694, and the mother of two children when the parents set sail.

THE SPELLING OF HIS NAME.—The name "Samuel Spear and Elizabeth, his wife," occurs on these records in 1733, in 1734 and 1737. The name Spear continues to occur numerously on these records in succeeding years, with varying Christian names, but nowhere else "Samuel and Elizabeth." And why not? They had removed to Canton, Mass., in 1739, where they remained all their subsequent life, and there died and were buried. That the above spelling Spear was a clerical error, we have absolutely conclusive evidence.

The compiler of this recollects it being said in his hearing, many years ago, that the son, John, of said Samuel was baptized in the "Salem Street Church," which is the same. A son to "Samuel and Elizabeth Spear" was baptized Oct. 23, 1737; it is known by the record in the old family Bible that he was born Oct. 17, 1737, in Boston. When Samuel first bought land in Canton, he is cited in the deed (on record in Boston) as of Boston. When he bought other land, in 1741, he is cited as "of Stoughton." Stoughton was divided in 1797, and its northern part made Canton. Samuel Spare sailed with two children. They are accounted for by the "burial" of one in Boston, while tradition says of the other, "died on the passage over."

Lastly, the name Spare has been confounded with Spear for 150 years, when written by others than themselves; and such spelling has been allowed to pass on important papers,—on the deeds above mentioned, on the rolls of Canton Minute Men, 1775, in the State House, Secretary of State's office. Until within the generation just past, their neighbors in Canton more often called them Spear than otherwise, and they let this pass. That it was written Spare by one person in Canton, in 1738, will be shown in these pages. It has always been so spelled by themselves. One of the grandsons of Samuel, however, adopted the spelling "Spear," and all his descendants, as these pages will show.

Samuel Spare came from Devonshire, as the compiler has it by tradition; this being a county of 700,000 people, it is not so specific as would be desirable and interferes with tracing his history in England. His wife was a London woman, her maiden name not ascertained.

THE NAME SPEAR.—This is a very numerous family in this country and of earlier arrival than ours. Many live in Quincy, Braintree, Boston and elsewhere. Many joined Christ Church after 1739. It is a curious set of coincidences that there was a Samuel Spear in Boston in 1796, as also a Samuel Spare, a John Spear, Jr., in 1808, and a John Spear, Jr., born Spare; and in Canton, in 1771 to 1777, a John Spear and wife, Mary, while there was also a John Spare ; and in 1746 a " John Spear " less than 16 years old, while there was a John Spare 9 years old. A petition is held by the writer for an article in the warrant for the remission of a tax paid by John Billings for the former, "he not being 16 years of age." It does not seem probable that this was John Spare, who, at his tender age, would not be living away from home—or, if so, could be mistaken for a boy actually 16.

OTHER SPARES THAN OURS IN THIS COUNTRY.—There is in Pennsylvania, especially Montgomery County, a much more numerous colony of Spares than ours. By a letter of enquiry addressed by the compiler to the editor of the Pottsville *Emporium*, in 1854, a letter was received from Charles G. Spare, of Garwood, Montgomery County, saying that his great-grandfather and great-grandmother (names not given) came from Germany about 1730 or 1732. His son Leonard, the grandfather of Charles, located at Upper Providence Township, Montgomery County, Pa. Leonard's sons were Philip, Nathan, Jonas (Charles' father), William and Samuel. Philip had three sons, Nathan eleven sons and two daughters, Jonas four sons and two daughters. In 1854 there were 200 persons of this name in said county alone. Some of these two stocks have occasionally encountered each other. The name is said to be not very rare in England and Germany. In Voltaire's Life of Charles XII we read of Count Axel Sparre.

CHRIST CHURCH IN BOSTON.—This was established in 1723, and the same structure and service in it remain to this day. The tower (probably the upper part) was blown over in 1804 and rebuilt. The church is on an elevated site in the north part of the city, and is celebrated as being the tower from which the lantern signal was displayed on the occasion of the embarcation of the British on the night of April 18, 1775, for the Charlestown shore—a signal to Paul Revere, already on that shore, ready to make his historical ride.* During the late centennial review of these historical points, there was much discussion in the Boston papers whether this was the church, there being another claimant in the field. After the subject was well canvassed, a conviction in its favor put the matter at rest, and the City Council voted $1100 to defray the expense of lettering and placing on its front a memorial tablet commemorating the lantern signal in appropriate words. The original Christ Church

---

* Read Longfellow's poem, " Paul Revere's Ride."

records have been so much worn and are of such a delicate and tender character that people could not consult them freely. They were kept in a bank vault, but the rector, Dr. Burroughs, was kind enough to consult them for the compiler, with the results here given. The city government has ordered them copied into substantially bound books, which are at the office of the City Registrar.

SAMUEL SPARE, RESIDENT OF BOSTON.—Nothing is known of the street of his residence. His occupation there can be pretty well surmised; that he was a trader, from the fact that when, in 1739, he bought twenty acres of land in Canton he paid "300 pounds, partly in money and partly in goods"—an extravagant price, unless it was paper money greatly depreciated. Tradition makes him a mariner in England; he calls himself a sawyer in his will. No occupation is given in five deeds granted. No doubt he was a sawyer in England, as he pursued that and farming in Canton. If he was a trader in Boston in February, 1738, he was able to take leave of his business, leave wife and an infant four months old, for the space of three months, as an old paper will show.

What was Samuel Spare's purpose in stopping three months in Canton, one year before he bought any land there, may possibly be conjectured: to clear up land which he had virtually bought, the delivery of the deed being a mere accident. He owned no place in Boston, so far as registry of deeds shows. In Boston he was a devout attendant, as was his wife, "upon all ye ordinances of the church," and, in removing to Canton, found himself in the neighborhood of his kindred church people which may have had something to do in attracting him.

There was no English Church in Canton then, but there was to be one, as we have a man "to lay its foundations." We observe that he goes to Canton in February, to stay three months—just long enough to have land ready for cultivation in the coming spring.

SAMUEL SPARE IN CANTON.—He removed to Canton in 1738 or 1739, and must have lived for 19 years in the house which he bought, with the 20 acres, of Elias Monk, Jr., not the 20 acres at the 13-milestone Spare House, for the only house which Samuel built on his land after 19 years' occupation he erected in 1758.

The lot was bounded north by the well-known Indian line and west by the Capt. John Tucker lane. This lane was the only public team road leading to Punkapog Village before 1765, and to the church, and to the nearest school (that at the town centre). There was a "path," later a team private road (at present Green Lodge street), passing by the house—most probably travelled by foot people going to church, which was a mile distant.

The site of this farm may now be recognized as passed through by present Green Lodge street, being the first arable land found after the lots immediately at Punkapog in going northwest from Punkapog Village about half a mile. The site of the Samuel Spare house, torn down in 1856, has been extinguished, being passed over by the newly straightened street in 1870. One of two wells remains, about eight rods west of house site, nearly filled by washed-in soil. Here Samuel cultivated the soil, and, no doubt, sawed plank out of the native forests for his neighbors. The writer has accounts of sawing by his son, 1762, at which date the father was 79 years of age. A fine but old orchard of apple trees was remaining in bearing order during the early years of the writer. The "lady-fingers," the "greasy-apples," the "double-apples" (nearly a third of them united like the Siamese twins), the "rattle-apples" (which, when ripe, would rattle their seeds, if shaken), the "sweet russets" and the "red russets." These varieties of apples the writer has never seen elsewhere. Only one of the apple trees remains to this day, which is, probably, 130 years old. Samuel bought three other small lots of land near by, and one of 10 acres, on the west side of Punkapog Brook, now belonging to William Horton.

He assisted, 1754, in founding Trinity Church, Canton, situated about a third of a mile southwest from Punkapog Village, where the cemetery now is. About 1793 it was moved and converted into a dwelling house; this was burned in 1874.

The site of this farm is in the valley of the Punkapog Brook. It had the advantage of more easy clearing, at that early day, as respects stones, the soil being the wash of the hills in the vicinity, and was thereby made relatively fertile. A few feet digging found water. But there was nothing eligible about the site for picturesque prospect or for sanitation. Toward the east, the ground rose gradually to an elevation of at least 150 feet, where is the school-house, shading out the rising sun. Four or five rods from the house, with these hills in one's rear, was the only place in town of echo known to the writer. Boys, driving the cows, were in the habit of amusing themselves in hearing their own voices a second time.

A monument, bearing the names of Samuel Spare and of three generations after him, in that cemetery, was erected in 1866. For a very full history of the church and rector, William Clark (1740-1815), see N. E.

Geneal. Register for January, 1875, by D. T. V. Huntoon, Esq., of Canton. The funeral sermon was preached by Rector Edward Winslow, without doubt in the church. The records of Clark show this.

His barn, after two removals, 1814 and 1829, now stands on the once Petingill place, opposite the old Doty Tavern. We have but few anecdotes of him. The writer heard his grand-daughter Elizabeth say that she "could just remember him." Gen. Nathan Crane, who died about 1830, very aged, was his neighbor. The General stated that he, a boy at the time, had witnessed his passionate dissatisfaction with one of his workmen, when he let fly his cane toward him to emphasize his meaning. There is no doubt Samuel was a sanguine, earnest man, devout, frugal, thrifty, of such stock that his descendants may reverence his memory, conscious that they have inherited something of his praiseworthy qualities. Once an Englishman, always an Englishman. He did not live to see the troublesome times of the Revolution or he could not have survived that struggle, bound up as he was in that English church, when its last rector was obliged to suffer indescribable indignities and flee the country.

RELICS.—An arm chair of large, square form, three of the legs of which went up to support the arm and back-rest, which, of a semi-circular form, went round horizontally about the height of the centre of one's back, was preserved to the middle of this century; a large family Bible, London, 1685, containing family record of his grandchildren, except a few (no deaths), also remained, and a half-dozen whip-saws, whose half-worn-away hard-wood handles showed their service, are all the writer remembers—except an elliptical bird's-eye maple table-top, reputed to have been "brought over" by the first pair, which, in 1832, was converted by Henry Fisher into a square stand, and now stands in the writer's office.

THE WIFE.—Her funeral sermon, to follow, gives interesting points, in which her character is shown as portrayed by her pastor. In her younger days her lungs must have been more effective. She spun flax, and, when one of her implements was missing, she would go out of her door, and, in language more forcible than polite to the ears of our day, would sing out, as a woman can, "She Billings! fetch home my distaff!" She Billings lived about 30 rods away, in what is known in our day as the Capt. John Tucker house. In her declining years Elizabeth's intellect failed. She would strike an attitude before her glass, and, adjusting her cap, would address her own reflection as a neighbor with the remark, "I am coming over to see you, pretty soon." She died at the age of 80—no definite record. She bore her last child Oct. 17, 1737, so far as known, which fact may be used to define her age somewhat. She was called a "London lady," whatever that may mean.

WILL OF SAMUEL SPARE.

In the name of God amen. The Twenty Second Day of april anno Domine 1767, I Samuel Spare of Stoughton in the County of Soffolk, within His majeftic prouince of the mafsachufsets Bay in New England, Sawyer, being very weak in Body but of perfact mind and memory Thanks be given to God therefore, Calling unto mind the mortality of my Body and knowing it is appointed unto men once to Die, do make and ordain this my Last will and Teftament. That is to say principally and first of all I giue and Recommend my Soul into the hands of God that gaue it and my Body I Recommend to the Earth to be buried in decant Chriftian buring acording to the Rites and Ceremonies fo the Church of England at the Difcretion of my Executors whome I injoin to have a Sermond preached at my Funeral Nothing Doughting at the general Refurriction I Shall Reciue the Same again by the atmighty power of God, and as touching such worldy Eftate where with it hath pleased God to blefs me with in this Life I giue demifs and difpofe in manner & form Folling

Imprimis I gaue and bequeath to Elizabeth my Dearly beloued wife The one half of my Eftate, Real personal and mouables for and During her natural life.

Itim. I gaue and bequeath to my well be loued son John Spare the other half of my Eftate he paying my Juft Depts and Funeral Charges for and During his natural life.

Itim I gaue and bequeath to my well beloued grandfon Samuel Spare Junr the one half of my Dwelling houfe togeather with Ten acres of Land Lying the weft side of punkapog brook in Stoughton aforefd he to come into pofsefsion of the primises at his grandmothers Decefe if he then be twenty one years of age, If not my son John Spare to improve it untill my grand fon is of age and att the Deceafe of my wife and Son John Spare I gaue and bequeath my whole Eftate to my grandfon Samuel Spare Junr to him and his heirs foreuer whome I in joyn to pay thirteen pounds sixteen shillings and eight pence in twelve months after the Deceafe of my wife & son or Intreft till paid to and for the ufe of the poor be Longing to the Church of England in this Town To be Let out upon Intreft and only the Intrift to be spent and if my grandfon Samuel Spare, Junr Should die and Leaue no child I gaue and bequeath my whole Eftate to my grand daughter Hannah Spare and her heirs foreuer on the fame condicons that I gave it to my grandfon Sam^{el} Spare Ju^r.

Itim I gaue and bequeath to my well beloued grand Daughter Hannah Spare Sixteen pound Lawfull money to be paid by my fon John Spare out of my Eftate at her arrival at the age of twenty-one years.

Itim. I do hereby conftitute make and ordain my well beloued wife & fon John Spare the Sole Executors of this my Last will & teftament, and I do hereby utterly Difallow Re-uoke and Difannul all and euery other former Teftament will Legacies and bequeft and Executors by me in any ways before Named willed and bequeathed

DESCENDANTS OF SAMUEL SPARE.

Ratifying and confirming this and no other To be my Last will and Teftament in witnefs whereof I have Hereunto set my hand and Seal the Day and year aboue written.   SAMUEL SPARE.

Sined Sealed published & Declared by the said Samuel Spare as his Laft will and teftament in the prefence of us the subfcribers.

JOSEPH BILLING,
TIMOTHY KENY,
SAMUEL BILLING.

A true Coppe of his said will who Deceafed July ye 5th, 1768, In the 85th year of his age.

the text of his funeral Sermon was There remaneth a reft for the people of God.

FUNERAL SERVICES OF THE WIDOW.—We give them from the original manuscript of the rector, Wm. Clark.

PRAYER BEFORE A FUNERAL SERMON,
(At the Burial of Elizabeth Spare),
OCT^R· 12, 1774.

Almighty and everlasting God who rulest in the armies of heaven above & among the Inhabitants of ye Earth beneath. There is none that may stay thine hand or say unto thee what Dost thou! We give thee the Glory of thy Divine perfections and acknowledge thine uncontrolable power in giving and Taking away, & when Thou w^t Rebukes dost chasten man for Sin by inflicting Death on ye progeny of Adam, we acknowledge the Justice of thy Dispensations & with all humility & refignation w^d Blefs thy Holy Name.

Lord Blefs our most Gracious Sovereign King George & all the Royall Family the Princes Lords and nobility of the realm. Endue them w^t Thy Holy Spirit, Enrich them with thine Heavenly Grace. Bless all the Bishops, Pastors and Teachers of thy flock, & to all thy people Give thine Heavenly Grace, especially to this Congregation here present, y^t with meak hearts and Due reverence &c.

We also Bless thy Holy Name for all thy Saints Departed this Life in thy Faith & Fear, Befeeching to give us grace So to follow their Good' Example y^t w^t Them we may be partakers of thine Havenly Kingdom.

And from the instances of Mortality Before us awaken to Such Lively apprehensions of & preparations for, our own Difsolution y^t when thou shall call us to Depart Hence our Souls may be presented without Spot before:—Teach us who Survive in this & other Like Daily Spectacles of Mortality to see how frail and uncertain our condition is & so to apply our hearts to that Holy & heavenly Wisdom while we Live here, as may in ye End Bring us to Life Everlasting. Thro the merits of † Thine only Son our Lord in whose comprehensive words we further call upon Thee. Our father &c . . .

AT MRS. [ELIZABETH] SPARE'S FUNERAL.
Live 3d p. 14.   Serm No 249 on Psal. 49:15.

Our aged and venerable sister whose remains are now Before us, has pafsed this Gloomy vail, & we trust has entered ye Joy of her Lord. After a long life Spent in a

†tian manner, she comes to her Grave as a shock of corn in the season & from her Blamelefs & †tian Deportment thro Life, according to our Best observation we have no reason to Doubt But that she is Beyond ye power of ye Grave or of Hell, and thro the merit of her almighty redeemer in whom she trusted & in whom she Believed received into his immediate presence as to her Spiritual Existence, & to the most Glorious Communion w^t her God & our God. The grave into which she will presently be Deposited, and which appears with So much horror to the Living as a dark and melancholy abode, is a calm & sweet repository to ye Dead, where they may rest undisturbed till ye Great Resurection morn^g, when they y^t Sleep in ye Dust shall awake and sing. w^t regard to the character of the Deceased tis presumed that most of my hearers know better than the Preacher; To whom I w^d say, whatever you observed in her virtuous and praiseworthy Imitate it with all y^r might. But if any thing vicious or unworthy, avoid it with all y^r care. To me she ever appeared Endowed with a peculiar innocency and simplicity of heart and having many years since left her native Land (with her worthy consort sometime since deceased) she brought with her a zeal for that religion which is there professed in primitive perfection, a religion which supported her in life & carried her Thro. Death & you who worship God wh'n these walls have been witnefses to her Devotion and piety and her strict attendance upon all ye ordinances of her savior, and How often has she struggled & panted for Breath and Strength to carry her to the House of God. My Breth^n. I am witness to what I say & under all ye pains and infirmities of old age she never forsook this place, till it pleased God in Great measure to Deprive her of her Discerning Capacity and lay her under a moral inability for his service. By ye Example of her presence and attendance in conjunction w^t her worthy consort (who helped Lay the foundation of this Building) she gave great Encouragement to the chh. of England which she loved while at ye same time she maintained a fervent charity to good men of every Denomination. She lived I may venture to say respected as a †tian & Died in Expectation of ye reward of immortality, and may you ye children and grandchildren of the Deceased Strive Earnestly strive to imitate ye pious and Laudable Example of your parents who have gone before you, that you may live respected on earth, and be sharers with y^m in ye honours of heaven. And now my Brethren let me Exhort you in ye words of ye apost. Be ye Followers of them y^t thro Fth & patience &c. . . . . This instance of mortality is a call to ye aged Be ye also ready,—alas it is but a little while & we must be carried to our Long home every one in his own order. The aged are continually dropping off the stage. Our Fathers where are they &c &c, a few years will carry both old and young into an immense and Boundlefs eternity where there shall be no more change. (see Dead 2d P. 14).

After residing 19 years in the house purchased with the place of Elias Monk, Jr., he built another probably on the same site.

THIS DWELLING HOUSE—about 22 ft. square—was constructed for two families, gambrel roofed, the two parts precisely alike as to situation and size. Only four rooms were on the lower floor, two of which were bedrooms. One division of the house was plastered, the other sealed;

the last, the east part. The house faced the south. The writer saw the "noon-mark" in the window. Over-head, were in full relief, appeared the chamber-floor sleepers, brown and dingy, with the smoke of nearly a century. These were native timbers, whose upper surface alone had been hewed. There were attached to these timbers overhead, wooden hooks, a native crotch, used for guns. The writer saw those of Elijah Howard hang thereon. The chimney stood at the common corner of the four rooms, giving a fire place to each. The face of each fire-place fronted toward the centre of each room ; the hearths triangular. Stairs from each bedroom met at a half-way landing and went up as one. The chamber was all one room, entirely unfinished, though with a smooth, good floor. The chimney, having no fire-place here, passed through in its naked, natural, brick-and-mortar simplicity. This large, whole chamber was doubtless utilized by the use of dividing curtains. The writer can never forget going up there with older boys, not suspecting any one in the house, and, looking behind the chimney, seeing an aged man there sitting, with long, flowing, gray hair. That was enough ; an instant stampede of us boys, as well the older as the writer, then five and a half years of age. The ominous words were whispered in his ear, "Old man! Skipper Kenney!" This man, David, died June 10, 1822. The clapboards on this house were of home make, about 10 feet long. It was once painted red, so as to get the name of the Red House. Not much paint remained visible at the end of the first fourth of this century.

We see by the will the house and lot were divised to son John and grandson Samuel. In 1789 this Samuel bought by quit-claim his father's half. On the death of the son in 1796, the father inherited the whole, which he held till his death. By will, 1814, he left the use of it to son James, "if he came to Canton to improve it," otherwise to this James' two sons, Samuel and James, Jr. Samuel died before being 21 when, by the terms of the will, that half was to be Elijah's, uncle of James, Jr. Well, to tell the whole story, this Elijah bought James, Jr.'s, half in 1829 and held it till about 1852, when he sold it to Capt. Wm. Shaller, who held it till 1882.

At the earliest period of the writer's recollection the then cultivated portion of the 20-acre purchase was nearly half good arable mowing land. How much of this was cleared for cultivation by Samuel Spare is unknown. His predecessor, or latter's father, also living near, was the first settler, from about 1704. By one of the three the land was first brought under cultivation. It is the writer's belief that the apple trees were set out by Samuel, and valuable they were, 50 or 60 in number.

DESCENDANTS OF SAMUEL SPARE.

Before the year 1831 it is doubtful if a plow had turned this soil for 40 or 50 years, except half an acre at Legget's corner; the general fate of land of ambiguous ownership—or owned by an aged man. Samuel Spare's lots afforded him plenty of wood and timber. The lot bought of Thomas Spurr in 1748, "on the west side of Punkapog brook," Samuel must have walled as it now appears, and somewhat cultivated; now gone back to forest growth. Very large oak trees were standing thereon till 1825. The writer remembers being one of two boys, who, with outstretched, united arms, endeavored in vain to clasp one—the original growth.

LIST OF NAMES—Of those in the church profession in May, 1767, [English Church, Canton,]—from the Boston *Gazette* of Aug., 1767: Samuel Spare, John Spare, Joseph and John Aspinwall, Edward Wentworth, Wm. Crehore, Daniel Waters, Noah Kingsbury, Hugh Knox, Samuel White, Richard McDaniel, John Martyn, Samuel Rusoe, Widow Arnold, Maj. John Shepard, Jonathan and Timothy Kenny, Henry Crane, Increase Leadbetter, Fitch Gibbons, Daniel Talbot, Matthew Blake; Jos. Aspinwall, clerk; Samuel Spare and Edward Wentworth, Jr., wardens in 1764; Timothy Kenny and John Spare, wardens in 1766; John Spare, warden in 1776.

Names of later date of actual communicants: Timothy Richards and wife, Wm. Brown, John Palmer, Wm. and Ruth Bussey, Mary Sanders, Sarah Sumner, Berry and Hannah Miller (negro), John Ness and wife, Timothy Richards; Ezekiel, Joshua, Margaret, Fisher and wife Chloe, and Jonathan Kingsbury; Eliakim Richards, Daniel Webb, Anna King, Capt. Scott, Sarah Cowell, Wm. Brown, Alex. Campbell, Ebenezer, Theophilus and Polly (Spare) Richardson, John and Charity Madden, Andrew and John Dunnigin, Sarah Will, Grace Jordan, Edmund and Elizabeth Quincy; Jonathan, Mary and Dorothy Taunt; Elizabeth Spare Fitzgerald, Edward Shail, Edward Taylor, Mr. Nehemiah and Philip Liscom, Isaac Royall, Edmund and Elizabeth Quincy, Mrs. Redman, Mrs. Blackman, Mrs. Badcock, [Joseph] Bemis, Abigail Leadbetter, Abijah and Dennis Blake, Thomas Crehore, Hannah Lewis, Daniel Gibbons, Abijah and Dennis Blake, Grace Jordan. Many of these were children confirmed.

Copied from the originals of old papers; the one following is on a piece of paper about 3 inches square:

DESCENDANTS OF SAMUEL SPARE.

I do hereby Certify that Samuel Spare and Edmund Condon are come to Live to my house out of the Town of Boston and are to continue here for about three months.
  Witness my hand this 27th day of feb'y 1737/8 JOHN KENY.

STOUGHTON, JUNE 4, 1744.

To the Selectmen of Stoughton:

Gentlemen—This is to inform you that I have taken Samuel Simson and Rebeckah Simson his wife to entertain them in my house.
                 SAMUEL SPARE.

Several others like this above.

1.

JOHN² (Samuel¹), m. Dec., 1757, Elizabeth, dau. of Hezekiah and Eunice (Torrey) Barber, of Boston; H. B. d. before 1744. She was b. July 13, 1740; d. in Canton Mar. 21, 1821. Eunice was from Scituate. She afterward married James Leonard, of Boston. *d. Dec. 1749*

  ch. i. HANNAH³, b. Oct. 27, 1758; buried Aug. 18, 1775.
2 ii. SAMUEL³, b. Sept. 24, 1760; d. ——, 1796.
   iii. EUNICE³, b. June 14, 1762; buried Aug. 28, 1775.
A iv. ELIZABETH³, b. Jan. 12, 1766; d. June 22, 1840.
3 v. JOHN³, b. Oct. 11, 1769; d. May 10, 1809.
B vi. POLLY³, b. Mar. 17, 1775; d. Sept. 6, 1814.
C 4 vii. JAMES³, b. Dec. 9, 1778; d. May 14, 1834.
D viii. MEHITABLE³, b. Sept. 30, 1780; d. Sept., 1833.
E ix. PEGGY³, b. Dec. 28, 1782; d. Oct. 19, 1848.
F 5 x. ELIJAH³, b. Feb. 20, 1785; d. Nov. 1, 1865.

The deaths of Hannah and Eunice, two oldest of three, sisters, of an interesting age, within ten days, must have been heart-rending to the family. The deaths are found in Rector Clark's diary. Nothing is transmitted of the cause of this mortality.

John² Spare was carried to Canton, an infant. As there was a school at Canton Centre, about one and a half miles distant, he must have attended it with many other children of the neighborhood. The writer has numerous originals of his handwriting. His father was stern in his discipline, and brought him up in obedience. The earliest anecdote handed down of him, is that when about 18 years old, John was returning from putting a yoke of oxen to pasture and bringing home the yoke on his shoulder, when he discovered he was followed by a bear. Thinking it was not necessary, under the circumstances, to be encumbered with a load, he threw it down. in order to facilitate locomotion. On looking back from a short distance he saw the last of the animal, smelling of and licking the suggestive yoke. This must have been on that now abandoned road leading over the Stone Bridge, and to the west of the bridge, and in 1755. The writer was told this anecdote by different grandsons of John, and 50 years apart, and it is undoubtedly true.

The year 1759 arrived. England had in hand the capture of Quebec and Canada. John and one of his neighbors, Jesse Tilson, joined the enterprise, in which New England was equally interested. They enlisted and sailed from Boston May 12 in a fleet of 30 vessels with supplies, cattle, etc., convoyed by a British man-of-war, and arrived, June 28, at the Isle of Orleans, opposite Quebec, which was a landing station for everything, powder, shot and shell, and cattle. This landing was some distance from the Battery. Their work was—certainly that of Tilson, who in his journal, now held by the writer of this, says "we"— carting to the Battery. This journal has daily entries from the sailing from Boston to the time of sailing to return to Boston on October 25, and in it are observations each day. The capture was on Sept. 18 One day, July 12, "a shot from the enemy killed two of our oxen and cut a spoke out of the wheel." On several days "we mowed wheat all day to make wads for the battery." One day they observed a fire-raft sent down by the French to burn the British vessels. "Aug. 8 our bateries set the lower town on fire and burnt down about a hundred houses." These two companions were not soldiers in the ranks, but workers in the commissary and ordnance departments. This journal is very interesting, but cannot well be quoted at length here. It will be seen by the dates that he left his wife and first infant, Hannah, at home. He resided always in the paternal homestead till he built elsewhere as to be stated.

He continued at home the business of farmer and sawyer. He and wife took all his children to church to be baptized, or this was done in his own house. This was done at the church until 1792, although there were no other services at church after June 11, 1776, a very suggestive date. The town had conditionally adopted the Declaration of Independence by action in town meeting six weeks before the United Colonies.

John Spare, who inherited his father's sentiments, and church associations, (that at Canton had been built, and partly maintained by the English Society for the Propagation of the Gospel in Foreign Parts), has been suspected of Tory proclivities almost to the last ditch, but as the Revolution was in men's minds, and in all American men's minds at some date, all that can be said is that it affected his mind later than some and much earlier than some, for where is there another instance like this: A father, aged 38, shoulder to shoulder with his own son, Samuel, aged 14 years, seven months in the ranks, marching as Minute Men on the memorable day of, or day after, the battle of Lexington, April 19, 1775, with 468 others, nine companies, from Stoughton and Stoughtonham. These Minute Men had been drilled two days a week. This quick rally of nine companies by night could only have been accomplished by the ringing of the bell and rapid riding over a large territory.

On May 26, 1775, his name is not reported by the selectmen in a list as "inimical to their country's cause," as those of four of his churchmen were.

Samuel[1] and John's names appear on a petition, very numerously signed in Feb., 1761, for an article in the warrant for a town meeting whereby the town is requested to allow the inhabitants of the town "who live north of the Punkapog brook," their share of school money for "having built a school-house and got a master to keep school." The writer holds the original petition, and it is important as showing that these people were bent on a school, although not required by law, and as showing the date of the first school-house in the present Blue Hill District. The second (that which is now a dwelling house in the rear) was built in 1798; remodelled in 1829. The present was built in 1846. The name of Samuel Spare is on a similar petition relating to school affairs, with date, 1742; also held by the writer.

John Spare lived in the paternal homestead till some time between 1775-80, when he purchased the John Kenney (1704-1759) site, it having thereon the old Salter-Kenney house, which he tore down and erected the present house and to this removed. It was at first a gambrel-roofed house, gable to the south, so shedding water east and west. About 1811 it was enlarged, extended seven feet west, the north projection added and the whole carried up two story.* Thomas Crane was the original builder, with, no doubt, Samuel[3] Spare an apprentice carpenter with him. The enlarging carpenter was John McKendry, with his brother William an apprentice, as the latter told the writer, and "Elijah Spare bossed the job." So the house now standing, forever marked as the 13th mile-stone site, is over a century old. There is no deed on record of John Spare's purchase of this place on Washington street of 20 acres; but he certainly

---

* Except the projection.

DESCENDANTS OF SAMUEL SPARE.

owned it in May, 1780, as the estate at the north was then "bounded on the south by land of John Spare." *

John Spare was in business in Boston (his family always in Canton) more than half his time, say from 1790 to 1805, sawing timber at lumber yards; industrious and saving always. This absence accounts for the non-appearance of his name in numerous lists of citizens, where one would expect to find it, as, for instance, in that on a petition for a division of the town in 1795. He does not appear to have accepted any prominent public office, except warden, the last one, and treasurer of the church. As a Minute Man he was probably not absent beyond a few days or weeks and this at Roxbury, near Boston, "at the lines." There is a tradition that he went as soldier in an important military expedition to Vermont or elsewhere; but it is so vague in the writer's knowledge that he can say nothing more about it. There is a story with it, however, but not the following.

As an anecdote, he was once solicited by an impecunious person for aid. He handed the supplicant half a dollar. The latter began to inspect it very carefully and finally asked if it were good. The giver said, "O, let me just take a look at it." Taking it he said, "So you don't like it? Well, now I like it," and put it back in his pocket to stay.

When his grandchildren were noisy in an adjoining room, he would chalk out on the floor and assign them their localities apart.

Of good constitution and excellent health, on his eightieth birthday he was at work in the field when he remarked that fact to his grandson, James, and said he should not live three years longer. On the last day of May, 1820, it being a holiday (Election Day), he drank ice-water on Boston Common. He was taken with sudden illness, necessitating his being taken to his Eliot street house. His death followed June 6, in Boston; buried in Canton.

At his burial the writer was taken by his mother to the grave and saw the coffin let down by ropes, she remarking that probably John would remember it. After arriving home John said to his mother, "I know how we can get grandpa again." "How?" "Why, put a rope around him and pull him up." He is remembered living, on two occasions.

The mile-stone which here speaks for itself has been a prominent mark for about a century.

It is four feet high, two feet nine inches broad, hammered in front and sides, natural rounded top and is hard, pink sandstone or gray-wacke

---

* Deed of heirs of John Davenport to Lemuel Davenport, Dedham.

of the region. Cut by nearest neighbor, Lemuel Davenport. The Canton Historical Society has paid it special respect by visiting it in a body.

13
Miles
To Bofton
1786
John Spare

●

Rector Clark's diary says that Elizabeth, wife of Samuel[1] was "about 80" at death.

Hezekiah Barber, in the latter part of his life, although he owned an estate in Dorchester and had lived there, lived in Boston. He was an "inholder" on the site of the present Adams House, previously the Lamb Tavern. He is reputed to have owned the inn site. At least his real estate was inventoried at £1322, while the "rates" paid on the Dorchester estate were only £2 5s. 6d., and all rates, 1744, £15 8s. 8d., so that the rates for Dorchester, where he owned numerous lots, was not one-sixth of all for 1744. There were three children besides Elizabeth. There ought to be found in Dorchester his gravestone, as was one paid for—£6. Debts paid, £674 3s. "old Tenor." Tradition has lived 140 years that one-fourth of Lamb Tavern site should have been Elizabeth's, as one-fourth of that in Dorchester became. Deeds at Dedham show the conveyance of this fourth by John Spare and wife, 1764.

She was a patient woman under much family suffering. Taken in an apoplectic fit and likely to fall on the hearthstone, she was caught and carried in her chair to her bed by son Elijah and grandson James Gerald, the writer a little witness and wonderer. Death followed. Thus the quite aged couple were taken away by brief sicknesses.

From the original of an old charge :

DOCHESTER.

Mr. John Spur to John Spare of Stoughton by Elizabeth Barber.
for the rent of one-quarter of the estate of Hezekiah Barber late dec
for ye year 1763   £3 6 8
for ye year 1764   £3 6 8
the rates exclusive.

STOUGHTON, MARCH ye 7 1766.

then Recieued of John Spare the sum of fiue shelling for work done on the Curch.

I Say Rec. by me.   STEPHEN CRANE, JUNR.

From the diary of Rector Wm. Clark :

Called and took a dish of tea at Mr. John Spare's.

Dec. 25, 1770. Christmas. Preach from Isaiah 53: 8, large audience; near twenty communicants. Dine at Mr. Spare's, with wife and Mr. Bemis.

STOUGHTON. MAY 11, 1772.

This is to give notice to the select men of said town that I have taken into my house Jonathan Tant his wife & child the 9th day of May instant from Milton.

JOHN SPARE.

John Spare's town tax for 1782 was £3 17s. 10d. ; of 180 names only five paid any more.

Eunice was dau. of James Torrey, of Scituate, who d. 1720. She m. Hezekiah Barber in 1721.

One lot of one acre, bought in 1742 by Samuel Spare of Elias Monk, was contiguous to and on south side of Indian line, nearly opp. school-house, bounded west by Washington street, and east by the extinct detour of the old road, "that passes near James Andrew's new house" (burnt, 1815). This lot continued to be owned by John till past 1790. In 1784 John bought the "Long Pasture" of Joseph Billings (1709-1789) situated in the rear of the school-house, contiguous to and on the north side of the Indian line, "for the just sum of 30 pounds," nine rods wide and running west far enough to make seven acres. On this was a dwelling house, where the old cellar now is, at the top of the hill 40 rods from W. street. In 1782 Natha'l. Kenney lived in it. John Spare removed this to the lot above mentioned, sold the lot to Benjamin Bussey, he to Laban Lewis in 1798, who lived there till 1816, when he removed it to make the rear part of the present Lewis-Hascom-Curtis house, second house further south. The remains of this cellar also now appear. The history of the digging of the well, 1803-7, on the site removed from—as shown in the preserved diary of Laban Lewis, by drilling many feet in the rock, using 45 bbls. of powder and 200 tons of stone in walling—is interesting. This diary mentions John Spare, Elijah Spare and John Gerald many times, John Gerald repeated this experience in digging two wells, 1832 and 1840, the lowest 14 feet being in solid rock, one on each of his two estates, 30 rods to the north. This is given for the benefit of any who propose to dig a well for the school-house. Readers at a distance, who know little of such a local matter in Canton, will excuse this digression, as a copy of this book is desired to be placed in the Canton town library.

Scarcely any history of persons or towns, in years long passed, is ever found disconnected from church matters. So let it be added here that John Spare, excommunicated, so to speak, without fault of his from his Canton Trinity Church by its own disestablishment, attended occasionally St. Paul's Church at Dedham, only six miles distant. He also had preachers of his own faith to hold services in his home, even down to the early years of this century ; so Mr. Montague, an aged gentleman, now in Boston, son of one such, told the writer. He further stated that the Spare name was a household word in his father's family, growing out of this relation.

Rector Wm. Clark, after spending some years in Nova Scotia, returned in 1795 to Quincy, where he lived the remainder of his life, with some exceptions, and where a tomb-stone marks his resting place.

IN MEMORIAM

Reverendi Gulielmi Clark, cujus
cineres sub hoc lapide sunt depositi,
olim quibusdam annis apud Dedham
Minstri episcopalis, at pro annis pluribus
ab officio sacerdotali per corporis infirmitates
Exclusi. Molestias varias et dolores per
vitam sustinuit, providentiæ divinæ
submissus et in spe ad vitam eternam
resurrectionis beatæ obit, Nov die IV

A. D., MDCCCXV. Æt LXXV.

Abi Viator, Disce vivere, Disce pati,
Disce mori ! In Christo mea vita latet,
mea Gloria Christus, et illius tandem
potestate omnipotente resurgam.

A physical infirmity prevented his holding service during these years. His Canton parishioner must have been a frequent visitor of him, with full knowledge of all his varied experiences, till his end. The distance was eight miles.

The old church, before its removal, had become considerably dilapidated. The clapboards had become loosened from the studding (it was not boarded beneath them), thus disclosing the sea-weed which had been the filling between the clapboards and inside wood sealing. Alexander Fisher (1780–1871) told the writer that he had seen swallows twittering about there, evidently having nests in the sea-weed.

It must have been on one of about the last baptisms held in the church, when the writer's father was one of a party of young candidates for this ordinance who assembled in it on an appointed day, but the bishop did not arrive for the purpose. Elijah was old enough to remember it.

Mr. Clark was a missionary of the English society mentioned to the three churches at Dedham, Stoughton, and Quincy. Residence mostly at Dedham while he praached.

2

SAMUEL[3] (John[2], Samuel[1]) m., Sept. 10, 1791, Betsey Hill, of Boston (called Elizabeth on administration papers of husband's estate, Boston), by Rev. Samuel West. She was probably dau. of William, as William Hill, Jr., was one of her bondsmen. She d. in Boston in 1796, but after her husband. There is a tradition of a child which did not survive the parents. Samuel[3] learned the carpenter's trade in Canton, no doubt of Thomas Crane. They owned, 1789, the Punkapog saw-mill together He worked a few years in Canton carpentering. He bought for $700, of Jesse Barber Wilcox in 1793, an estate in Boston, cor. of Eliot and Warren, now Warrenton street, on which was a wooden one-story dwelling-house on Eliot street and a carpenter shop on the corner. Here he lived, worked and died after his removal to Boston.* The shop, descending in the family (till 1868), became a grocery store occupied by one Francis for many years; replaced by a brick building in 1828; house replaced by brick three-story in 1834. Eliot street being widened on south side about 1870, only that estate, now of about 10 feet front on Warrenton

---

* See pages 9, 12 and 16.

and many more feet on Eliot, represents old site. His signature is now found only on an old receipt, by which it appears he made in Canton a coffin for 9s. for Dr. Esty in 1789. His chest of tools was in Canton as late as 1850.

The widow was appointed his administratrix, but, dying before settlement, his father, John, was made adminstrator *de bonis non*.[*] The wife of Samuel *Spear* cotemporary with him was Lydia Henchman.

3

JOHN[3] SPEAR (John[2], Samuel[1]) b., Canton : went to Boston young : "Baptism, 1769, Sunday, Nov. 12. John, son of John Spare of Stoughton. In his own house after evening services :" m. Mrs. Mary [Barnard], widow of Peter Emerson, with one child, a dau., who m. a Dolliver, of Boston, and whose children now living are Capt. James M. and Capt. Peter Emerson Dolliver and sisters, of Somerville and Auburndale.

Their mother lived to be 84, dying in San Francisco ab. 1878—a woman of remarkable gifts. John[3] is believed to have been a carpenter. He d. May 10, 1809, and was buried in the cemetery south end of Boston Common. He lived on "Frog lane," now Boylston street. opp. Boylston market. Death found in the files of the *Boston Independent Chronicle*, "funeral to be Sunday at his late residence Frog lane ; relatives and friends invited to attend without further notice."

The wife of the John Spear, Jr., of Boston, who d. June, 1808, aged 29, cotemporary with him, was Sally. Probate papers of this one, Boston. No relative of ours.

  ch i. WILLIAM[4] M., b. May 13, 1804 : d. Dec. 29, 1880.
   ii. JOHN[4] D., b. Feb 7, 1806 : d. Aug. 10, 1882.

WILLIAM[4] M. SPEAR (John[3], John[2], Samuel[1]) m. . . Sarah Jennings, b. Boston, who d. Aug. 10, 1882. He was born in Boston : went a young man to Philadelphia, where he continued all his subsequent life and died.

---

[*] Inventory and other papers in Probate, Boston.

DESCENDANTS OF SAMUEL SPARE.

    ch. i. OLIVE[5], b., . . . ; d. ab. 1849, unm.
       ii. SARAH[5], b., . . . ; d. ab. 1863 at Philadelphia, unm.
      iii. WILLIAM[5], b., . . . ; d. July 2, 1863. KILLED IN THE BATTLE OF GETTYSBURG, second day of fight.
      iv. CHARLES[5] W., b., . . . ; m., . . . Charles is living, with four children, and until recently at Philadelphia. He has changed his residence to "on east." He has been a travelling merchant.

JOHN[4] D. SPEAR (John[3], John[2], Samuel[1]) m., Dec. 25, 1831, Mary Schneider. She was b. Sept. 10, 1810; d. Feb. 6, 1874. Printer at Boston; dealer in paints and oils, lived at 917 S. 17th street, Pa.

    ch. : ELIZABETH[5], FRANCES[5], ABIGAIL[5], MARY[5], EMILINE[5], WILLIAM[5] M., and MIRIAM[5], who all d. in infancy, and
      viii. THEODORE[5] D., b. June 11, 1835; l. Pa.
       ix. ALBERT[5], b. Sept. 15, 1837; d. ab. June 20, 1874.
       x. JOHN[5] D., Jr., b. April 25, 1840; d. same day.
      xi. ELLA[5], b. June 23, 1847.
     xii. ANN[5], b. . . ; l. 1883.

Ella m. Wesley Burgess; have (1881) one ch., Wesley Burgess, Jr.; l. 917 S. 17th street, Pa. Ann m. Christian Hansen (live, 1881, Pa. ?).

THEODORE[5] D. SPEAR m., Dec. 1, 1859, Frances Catherine Rupp; l.

    ch. i. HARRY[6], b. Dec. 28, 1865.

These are living at 1811 S. 5th street, Phila.

ALBERT[5] D. SPEAR m., first, Lilla Cobb, died . . .

    ch. i. Child; d. in infancy.
      ii. GERTRUDE[6], b. . . .; living.
m., second, Helen Lawton, who is l.
    ch. iii. MIRIAM[6], b. . . .
      iv. HELEN[6], b. . . .
       v. ALBERT[6], these three living 1881.

Albert[5] D. was injured at the burning of his store. This is supposed to have been cause of death.

4

JAMES³ (John² Samuel¹) m., first, Elizabeth, dau. of James and gr. dau. of Hezekiah Barber ; she b. June 10, 1780 ; d. April 22, 1810.

    ch. i.   ELIZA⁴, b. April 4, 1799 ; d. July 7, 1877. Part II.
        ii.   SAMUEL⁴, 1st, b. May 1, 1801 ; d. March, 1821.
        iii.   HARRIET⁴, b. Mar. 4, 1804. Part II.
        iv.   EMILY⁴, 1st, b. Mar. 17, 1806 ; d. Mar 7, 1819.
        v.   JAMES⁴, b. Apr. 24, 1808 ; d May 14, 1854.

m., second, Feb. 14, 1813, Mary McCormack.

        vi.   WILLIAM⁴, ⎫ twins, b. Dec. 30, 1813, and both d.
        vii.   HENRY⁴, ⎭   Jan. 2, 1814.
        viii.   BAYARD⁴, b. Aug. 22, 1815 ; d. Aug. 30, 1866.
        ix.   SARAH-CROWE⁴, b. Apr. 27, 1817 ; d. Jan. 21, 1853.
        x.   JOHN-CLARK⁴, b. Mar. 7, 1819 ; l.
        xi.   SAMUEL⁴, 2d, b. Mar. 15, 1821 ; d. Mar. 5, 1855.
        xii.   FRANCIS-WAITE⁴, b. Apr. 29, 1823 ; d. Jan., 1852.
        xiii.   ELIZABETH⁴, b. Sept. 25, 1825 ; d. June 9, 1866.

m., third, Sept. 13, 1827, Catherine Milby, who d. Nov., 1856.

        xiv.   CAROLINE⁴, b July 6, 1828 ; d. Jan. 5, 1877
        xv.   CATHERINE-WHITSLE⁴, b. Aug. 20, 1831 ; living unmarried in Saxonville, Mass.
        xvi.   EMILY⁴, 2d, b. Apr. 27, 1834 ; living in Smyrna, Del.

Mary, dau of Arthur and Sarah McCormack, was a native of the north of Ireland; came to this country in 1798 with her father and mother, she being then about 10 years of age. She d Feb. 17, 1827.

Emily, 1st, was a girl of remarkable religious impressions. After her early death, the "Memoirs of Emily Spare," written by her minister, Mudge or Murch, was published by the Methodist Book Concern, for Sunday school libraries.

James³ Spare was b. in Canton, went a young man to Boston. Early married, settled in Boston, owned land in S. Boston. His house, which he owned, was on Dorchester avenue, probably near where the Wire Works now are. In 1808 he was a fire engine man of Co. No. 11. His diploma of membership, framed, was preserved for 50 years. He does not appear to have learned a fixed trade, which, by a letter, he wished he had; resided in South Boston till Sept. 21, 1811, when, embarrassed by the recent loss of his wife, and a mortgage on his place, which, as he wrote in a letter "must soon be sold to pay one-half of his debts at one-fourth of its value," he suddenly struck out to begin elsewhere life anew, leaving behind his five children at places found for them. It seems he went to Cantwell's Bridge, Delaware, where he resided nearly till his death. Died at Mt. Pleasant. He was remarkable for the tact he showed in various mechanical undertakings, moving buildings, planning and building bridges and wharves. At one time he carried on a fanning mill manufacture, and blacksmith and wagon shop. He was prominent in the community, and stood high in the esteem of all who knew him for his candor and unflinching integrity. As a presiding officer at public meetings of citizens, he showed a dignified presence and impartiality in his decisions. A Federalist in politics. In the troublesome days of the anti-slavery struggle he maintained unflinchingly the cause of the slave— that in a slave State, and with the general concurrence of his fellow-citizens against him. "He was stern and almost unapproachable, but," says a son, "we all loved, honored and esteemed our father."

"I want all my little bumble-bees to live undisturbed," said he one day while he was hewing timber, to the neighboring boys, as a cooler to their enthusiasm, as they were trespassing on his grounds and enticing his own boys away from their duties to join them in chasing the little winged creatures. "I have none too many bumble-bees."

The above letter, preserved, shows fine tact and correctness in literary composition. James[3] died at Mt. Pleasant, after one week's illness.

JAMES[4] (James[3], John[2], Samuel[1]) m. first, 1836, Ruth Titcomb, of a family long and well known many years, of Newburyport, Mass. She d. 1850.

    ch. i. ABIGAIL-CRANE[5], b. Jan., 1837. Part II.
       ii. CECELIA-KENT[5], b. Jan., 1839; d. 1841.
      iii. ELIZA-TITCOMB[5], b. Jan., 1841. Part II.
      iv. SARAH-LAMBERT[5], b. Feb., 1843. Part II.

m., second, Jane Mead, April 2, 1853 ; l. Galena.

    ch. v. JAMES-BARBER[5], b. Jan., 1854 ; d. May 15, 1860.

James[4] staid with his Uncle Elijah at Canton till 16 years of age; in 1824 went to Boston, learned the carpenter's trade with White of Tilesten street. Except a year or two he worked at his trade in Boston, shop on Hawley place, HOBART & SPARE. In 1836, under contract with certain persons to put up buildings, he went to Galena, Ill., and there continued as carpenter and lumber dealer till his death. Studious, fond of reading, in all leisure moments, general history and everything useful.

Industrious, frugal, he earned a competency, and was by every one esteemed. This is written on a mahogany desk made by him ab. 1830. The writer loved him as a brother.

James was Elder in the Presbyterian ch. at Galena, and tenor singer in the choir for years. A strong anti-slavery man and one of the officers of the underground railroad. His record as to church and school work was equal at least to that of his ancestors.

BAYARD[4] (James[3], John[2], Samuel[1]), m., Sept. 20, 1840, Mary Jane, dau. of Joseph Moore, of Ellsworth, Me.

    ch. i.   GEORGE-ARTHUR[5], b. Aug. 2, 1841 ; d. Dec. 5, 1874.
    ii.   CECELIA-KENT[5], b. Dec. 28, 1842. Part II.
    iii.   MARY-FRANCIS[5], b. Nov. 27, 1845. Part II.
    iv.   ELIZA-BOWDEN[5], b. Jan. 21, 1847 ; unm.
    v.   HARRIET-ESTY[5], b. Oct. 9, 1848 ; d. July 11, 1850.
    vi.   JAMES-BAYARD[5], b. Oct. 1, 1850 ; unm.

Bayard[4] was b. at Cantwell's Bridge, Del., whence, before 1840, he came to East Boston, where he married, settled and died, and where his widow and children continue to reside, except the Sanborn family, which r. in North Beverly. He was a carpenter ; generally esteemed ; bur. Woodlawn Cem. ; house at 108 Putnam street.

GEORGE-ARTHUR[5] m., Oct. 3, 1863, Octavia Southgate, dau. of James Sweetsir, of East Boston. She is living at East Boston.

    ch. i.   HARRIET-CLARICE[6], b. May 18, 1864 ; l. unm.
    ii.   JAMES-ARTHUR[6], b. June 5, 1870 ; l.

He, G. A., was a printer in Boston.

James-Bayard[5] is in the mercantile business, Boston.

JOHN[4]-C. (James[3] John[2] Samuel[1]) m., Nov. 12, 1840, Hetty Gallaher, who was b. in Carlisle, Pa., Sept. 23, 1823, and d. Aug. 18, 1881. High tributes to her worth and virtues and works appeared in the Galena papers, contributed by her many associates.

    ch. i.   SAMUEL-ARTHUR[5], b. Oct. 27, 1841, in Galena.
    ii.   MARY-CATHERINE[5], b. June 1, 1846 ; d. Nov. 6, 1848.

DESCENDANTS OF SAMUEL SPARE. 27

  iii. CORA-LUELLA[5], b. June 25, 1850; l. She was m.
Sept. 19, 1876, to David Sheean, a lawyer of Galena;
no ch. (1884). She was b in Utopia, O.
  iv. EUGENE-OLIVER[5], b. July 12, 1853, in Utopia; m.
Sophia Comstock, Sept. 5, 1876. Studied law, but at
present is a R. R. station agent near Chicago; no ch.
1884.

d. Nov 6 1889

SAMUEL-ARTHUR[5] m., first, Dec. 19, 1867, Lydia Warner, of Jo Daviess Co., Ills., who d. Feb., 1874.

  ch. i. JOHN-EDGAR[6], b. Mar. 17, 1869, near Leon, Decatur Co., Ia.
    ii. GEORGE-ARTHUR[6], b. May 4, 1871, in Jo Daviess County, Illinois.

m., second, April 23, 1880, Mary Michaels, of Colesburg.

  ch. iii. HETTY[6], b. Aug. 1, 1881.
    iv. Daughter[6], b. Oct. 11, 1883.

S. A. lives on a farm near Manchester, Delaware Co., Ia., farmer. S. A. and L. W. had one ch., unnamed; d. day of birth.

John-Clark[4], b. at Cantwell's Bridge, Newcastle Co., Delaware. Delaware being a slave State, the facilities for obtaining an education were very limited to children of parents not in affluent circumstances. His whole time at school did not exceed six months. He was taught to read and write by an older brother and sister. At his father's death, being then only 15 years old, he was thrown entirely upon his own resources to make his way in the world; bound himself an apprentice to Joseph C. Griffith, to learn the carpenter's trade, he agreeing to give him one month's schooling a year during the apprenticeship, or till he should be 21 years of age. This continued three years, when Mr. Griffith quit the carpenter's trade, and took up pump-making, keeping John at that and hiring him out to other parties by turns.

Objecting to this, and finding Mr. Griffith of an overbearing and exacting nature, a breach was made which could not be healed, and he appealed to the Orphan's Court asking a discharge from his indentures, examining witnesses and pleading his own case. This discharge was granted Sept. 21, 1837. He worked at Wilmington till April 21, 1838, when he started for Galena, Ill., at which place he arrived May 11, where he has spent most of his time since, except eight years farming. He worked 22 years at his trade, but later in the sale of agricultural implements and dealing in hides and pelts. Losing his wife in 1881, he retired from business.

He was alderman of the city of Galena for 1859, 1869 and 1876; was collector of West Galena, supervisor from West Galena and chairman of the County Board of Supervisors one year. Has been several times delegate to State conventions, chairman of Jo Daviess County delegation to the State convention in 1880, held at Springfield, Ill. Was chairman of the town, county and congressional conventions the same year, and was unanimously recommended by his county convention for State Senator. Was chairman of the committee on procession in the great Centennial celebration, 1876, and their treasurer and auditor. A man of strictly temperance habits, never using tobacco in any form, much of his time has been given to temperance work as speaker. An eventful life with many vicissitudes!

SAMUEL[4] SPARE (James[3], John[2], Samuel[1]) m., Mar. 23, 1847, Eliza, dau. of Abraham and Sarah (Thomson) Enos. She is living at Odessa, Delaware. She was b. Feb. 21, 1821.

    ch. i. THOMAS-ABRAHAM[5], b. Oct. 23. 1849; d. July 23, 1850.
    ii. JAMES-SAMUEL[5], b. Apr. 30, 1851; d. June 23, 1851.
    iii. MARY-ELIZA[5], b. June 20, 1853; d. Sept. 24, 1853.
    iv. SAMUEL-ENOS[5], b. Sept. 27, 1854; unm. (1884).
    v. SALLY-THOMSON[5], b. Sept. 13, 1855.

Sally-Thompson Spare and William D. Howell were m. Mar. 29, 1883. He is a farmer.

Samuel-Enos Spare is living in Philadelphia, 1884, employed at 520 Arch street.

Samuel[4] was b. at Cantwell's Bridge; was bound to Doughton & Miller to learn the carriage painting business. He was at East Boston for a time where he bought land, and subsequently moved to Delaware.

FRANCIS-WAITE[4] SPARE (James[3], John[2], Samuel[1]) m., Mar. 31, 1842, Sarah Jane Price, who was b. Mar. 12, 1827.

    ch. i. ELIZABETH[5], b. May 26, 1843. Part II.
    ii. MARY-ANN[5], b. Mar. 28, 1845; d. Mar. 5, 1849.
    iii. MARGARET[5], b. May 6, 1847. Part II.
    iv. MARY[5], b. Aug. 10, 1849; d. Sept. 20, 1850.
    v. JAMES-FRANCIS[5], b. Aug. 1851.

JAMES-F.[5] m., Mar. 2, 1876, Phebe McMullen.

    ch. i. DORA-ANNA[6], b. Oct. 11, 1883.

James F. and mother are living in Council Bluffs, Ia.

Francis Waite learned the shoemakers' trade of David McKee. He afterward settled in Iowa, where his widow remains.

5

ELIJAH[3] (John[2], Samuel[1]) m., March 31, 1812, Sally, dau. of Noah and Olive (Shepard) Clapp, of Norton, Mass., by Rev. Pitt Clark. She was b. Aug. 17, 1789, in Norton ; d. Dec. 14, 1863, in South Boston. (Noah was son of Samuel, of Samuel, of Thomas, of Thomas ; this brings it to 1633, settlement of Dorchester.) A woman devoted to duties of the family ; member of the Baptist Church of Canton, then of South Boston.*

    ch. i. ELIJAH[4], b. Feb. 13, 1813 ; d. Feb. 28, 1869.
        ii. GALEN[4], b. April 11, 1815 ; d. March 1, 1867.
        iii. JOHN[4], b. Nov. 13, 1816 ; l.
        iv. EDWIN[4], b. Oct. 6, 1818 ; d. Jan. 30, 1840.
        v. NANCY-CLAPP[4], b. Sept. 12, 1820 ; d. July 13, 1849.
        vi. SARAH-JANE[4], b. April 29, 1822 ; d. Aug. 11, 1883.
        vii. ELIZABETH-BARBER[4], b. Feb. 15, 1824 ; d. Oct. 13, 1881.
        viii. ALMIRA-STEVENS[4], b. Nov. 1, 1825 ; d. Aug. 24, 1830.
        ix. SAMUEL[4], 1st, b. Oct. 27, 1827 ; d. Feb. 28, 1828.
        x. LOUISA-MARIA[4], b. April 23, 1829 ; d. May 11, 1865.
        xi. SAMUEL[4], 2d, b. Jan. 27, 1831 ; d. Feb. 17, 1832.

Elijah[3], born in Canton, at the 13th-milestone house, owned it and the 20 acres, and 70 or 80 acres in his vicinity, and resided there till 1850. He, 1808, learned the wheelwright's trade of Michael Shaller, of Canton, which he followed till 1823, when he abandoned it. Then followed the business of farmer and sawyer till 1842, after which he did no active bodily labor. Removed to South Boston in 1850, where he had built a few houses, on northeast corner of B and Sixth streets, on

---

* See Clapp Family in America.

land which he had bought in 1806 of brother James : 9000 feet for $150. He had been Selectman of Canton, and Representative to the General Court, 1830, 1831: Was very stern and severe toward his children, but provided well. Of sanguine temperament, the great principle of his character was impressing uncompromising industry of every body controlled by him. Was anxious that his children should improve all advantages for education. Several of his orphan nephews found comfortable homes with him. He would make and repair the old style of cider-mill, and move buildings, as did his father and brother James. "A substantial man," said Dea. Houghton. A member of the Baptist ch. in Canton and in South Boston. Died in South Boston. Buried at Canton with wife.

ELIJAH[4], (Elijah[3], John[2], Samuel[1]) m., first, Feb. 4, 1840, Elizabeth, dau. of Aaron and Sarah (McKendry) Everett, of Boston, by Rev. Dr. Daniel Sharp. She d. Jan., 1854.

- ch. i. SARAH-ELIZABETH[5], b. Nov. 14, 1840.
- ii. MARIA-EVERETT[5], b. April 7, 1842 ; l. unm.
- iii. EMILINE[5], b. ab. 1844, d. aged 6 months.
- iv. ANTOINETTE[5], b. Jan. 15, 1847 ; d. Aug. 4, 1873.
- v. EMMA[5], b. July 27, 1851 ; l. unm.

m., second, Martha Emerson, who is living, Cambridge.

- ch. vi. ARTHUR-ELIJAH[5], b. Nov. 27, 1857.
- vii. JESSIE-MARY[5], b. Jan. 18, 1759 ; l.
- vii. GEORGE[5], b. . . ; d. infant.
- viii. ALANZO[5], b. . . ; d. infant.
- ix. MARTHA[5], b. . . ; d. at 6 months.

Elijah[4], born at Canton, attended, as did all his brothers and sisters, the school near by ; learned the carpenter's trade of John McKendry, of Punkapog, which he subsequently followed in Boston (Wingate & Spare, Pleasant street) ; bought land and built a house on Marion street, which he soon after sold to Lewis Wentworth. On marriage he kept house in Canton, opposite to Cherry Tavern. In 1843 he removed to East Cambridge, Thorndike street, bought land and built a house next west of his residence. He pursued a manufacturing business on Gore street till his death, but he had been failing in health for two years before his death, which was by apoplexy. He and his wife are buried at Spruce avenue, Mt. Auburn. He was executor of his father's estate without bonds, required by the will. He was always frugal and industrious and earned a competency.

Maria^5 E. is, and has been for several years, keeping school in Cambridge. She has made a residence in Germany for a year.

ARTHUR-ELIJAH^5 m., Sept. 28, 1881, Dora Anderson, of East Cambridge ; r. in Cambridge. He is in the mercantile business, Boston.

    ch. i. Daughter, b. . .

GALEN^4 (Elijah^3, John^2, Samuel^1) m., first, Nov. 26, 1844, Sarah Ann, dau. of Elijah Briggs, then of Canton. She was b. in Foxboro ab. 1824 and d. in Roxbury May 6, 1858. E. B. was b. 1798 ; d. 1880. She was a devoted woman ; obituary in *Christian Watchman*.

    ch. i. GEORGE-EDWIN^5, b. Aug. 26, 1845.
        ii. SUSAN-CARPENTER^5, b. July 18, 1847 ; d. May, 1857.
       iii. CHARLES^5, b. Sept., 1855 ; d. May , 1857.
       iv. SAMUEL^5, b. Aug. 10, 1853.

m., second, July 4, 1860, Ellen-Matilda, dau. of Simeon Ames Dean, of Norton ; he was b. 1810 and is living. 1880. Ellen survives her husband and is rem. to Albert Edgecomb ; lives in South Boston, with two daughters. No. ch. with G. S. She was b. Nov., 1839. Her mother d. May 16, 1870, aged 53.

Galen^4 attended the school at Canton ; later the Pierce Academy, Middleboro. He kept school in West Dedham, and on Milton Hill, 1842. He kept store at South Canton, FRENCH & SPARE, 1837-41. In 1841-42 he went to Indiana and bought produce to bring east. At marriage he kept house in same h. with his father, Canton, four or five years ; assisted his brother Elijah in business while continuing the farm at Canton. About 1851 bought the paternal homestead, and was collector of taxes one year. Not liking farming, he sold out to John Gerald, present owner ; moved to Roxbury in 1855, where he kept store in Gould's block, Bartlet street, till ab. 1864, when, after a year in the Armory at Springfield, he moved to South Boston, where he resided till death, assisting his father, now aged, in care of real estate.

He and first wife were members of the Dudley street Baptist ch., Roxbury ; both are buried at Forest Hill Cemetery, where there is a granite shaft as monument. He was a life member of the Home Missionary Society.

GEORGE-EDWIN^5 (Galen^4, Elijah^3, John^2, Samuel^1), b. in Canton ; m., first, Mary J. Larrey, Dec. 27, 1871. She d. Feb. 23, 1874. She was b. Nov. 24, 1846. M. J. L. was of Springfield.

  ch. i. ROBERT-HILDRETH[6], b. June 1 1873.

m., second, May 15, 1879, Lucy Merwin, dau. of George and Phebe (Merwin) Cook, of New Haven.

  ii. AGNES-MAY[6], b. Nov. 24, 1881.
  iii. GEORGE-COOK[6], b. Mar. 28, 1883.

G. E. S. commenced to work in his father's store in Roxbury as clerk ; thence went to Waltham to learn watch-making. After two years went to Springfield and worked a year in the Armory ; thence went to Chicago in 1864 as bookkeeper, then salesman in a large stove manufactory. Removed to Albany, N. Y., in the employ of the same firm July 5, 1871 ; was married while there. Next removed, Oct. 3, 1872, to New Haven where he became a member of the firm of Snell, Spare & Co.. carriage manufacturers; sold out his interest in this concern in Jan., 1877, and became interested in the carriage hardware business for two years. In 1879 was one of the incorporators of the Boston Buckboard Company of New Haven, Ct.. who manufacture about 2000 light pleasure carriages of all descriptions annually ; was elected secretary and business manager of this company on its formation and still holds the position. Residence, cor. of Davenport avenue and Vernon street.

SAMUEL[5], b at Canton ; m., Feb. 2, 1881, Alice, dau. of Francis and Ann (Rotch) Drake, of Mansfield.

  ch. i. FRANCIS-GALEN[6], b. May 18, 1882 ; 1.

S. S. learned the electrotype art at Albany and resided and worked there several years. Since then he has followed this art in Boston several years at 178 Devonshire street, residing now and for a few years past at 17 Mercer street, South Boston.

JOHN[4] (Elijah[3], John[2], Samuel[1]) m., July 12, 1846, Susan-Vigneron, widow of Benjamin Mason, and dau. of Mary-Vigneron (Weaver), of Long Plain, and Edward Bennett, of Montpelier, Vt. E. B. d. 1835. M. V. B. b. Feb. 4, 1802, at Newport ; d. Jan. 13, 1882, at New Bedford.

  ch. i. SARAH-LOUISA[5], b. Aug. 15, 1847.
  ii. JOHN-VIGNERON[5], b. Oct. 28, 1849.

DESCENDANTS OF SAMUEL SPARE.

   iii. JAMES-EDWARD⁵, b. Dec. 28, 1853; d. Jan. 10, 1854.
   iv. ELIJAH-ERIC⁵, b. Dec. 28, 1853; d. Feb. 5, 1854.
   v. SUSAN-FLORA⁵, b. Dec. 23, 1855.
   vi. WALTER-VERNON⁵, b. Dec. 16, 1860; d. Oct. 1, 1863.

JOHN⁵ V. m., Feb. 20, 1879, Hattie Maria, dau. of Capt. Andrew and Olive (Underwood) Snow, of New Bedford, by Rev. Matthew C. Julien. She was b. Sept. 23, 1855, at Harwich, Cape Cod.

   ch. i. CHESTER-VIGNERON⁶, b. Jan. 18, 1883.

John⁵ V. attended the Grammar and High schools of New Bedford; was apothecary in the Navy from July 7, 1865, till April, 1866, on steamers Mahaska and Yucca; was clerk in New Bedford Post Office 1866-1869. Is a merchant in dry goods in New Bedford since 1872; store at N. E. cor. County and High streets. House and lot S. W. cor. of Union and Arch streets.

Sarah⁵ L. is a school teacher since 1866 in New Bedford; since 1876 of the Parker street Grammar school. A graduate of New Bedford High school, 1866.

Susan Flora⁵ has been a teacher in New Bedford since 1874; since 1878 of the Parker street Grammar school. A graduate of New Bedford High school, 1873.

John⁴, compiler of this work, was b. in Canton; attended the common school near by; when large enough worked on the farm. In 1833 attended the Randolph Academy; in 1834, Amherst Academy; entered Amherst College Oct., 1834, graduated, A. B., 1838, A. M., 1864; studied medicine and graduated, M. D., at Harvard University in March, 1842. Commenced practice in East Milton May, 1842, but Jan., 1845, removed to Acushnet (Long Plain) and practiced; thence to East Freetown in 1846; thence to New Bedford, 1852, where he has since resided. In the Civil War was surgeon of the U. S. ship Release, which sailed April 23, 1862, to the Mediterranean, was nine months on this cruise; in 1863 made a second voyage to Cadiz, Spain. Continuing in the service, he was afterward on the blockade of Wilmington and Charleston in the U. S. steamer Cambridge in 1864-65; in 1865-66 was in the Gulf squadron on steamers Mahaska and Yucca; resigned July, 1866. Was a member of the New Bedford School Committee 1871-77. Published, 1864, a treatise on Differential Calculus; in 1868 was author of prize essay of the Massachusetts Medical Society. Has been since 1867 sole medical examiner for New Bedford of the Ætna Life Insurance Co. Is a Fellow of the Massachusetts Medical Society and of the American Academy of Medicine. Residence, 5 Arch street, New Bedford; office, cor. Purchase and Elm streets. Wife Susan V. b. Dec. 30, 1823, at Acushnet.

Edwin[4]. unm., was feeble from earliest boyhood. He never could run and play as his fellows did. Lived at home in Canton; went to school. In Dec., 1839, hoping to be benefited, he sailed from Boston for Charleston, S. C., where he arrived, but, as there was varioloid on board of the sailing vessel, it was quarantined, and, although he had gone into the city, he was required to go to quarantine hospital, Morris I., where he died ostensibly of varioloid; but he was nearly in the last stages of consumption when he left home, and by no method or place of residence could have survived a year. His painted portrait, 1839, by Dickerman, of Canton, remains with the writer, and his last letters from South Carolina.

James Barber, father of Hezekiah, was living in Dorchester in 1709; d. ab. 1720.

James Barber, son of Hezekiah, m. Margrett Robertson, Mar. 26, 1775. He d. Aug. 30, 1800, aged 57 years; she, Sept. 20, 1795, aged 36 years.

The site of Hezekiah's homestead in Dorchester, probably the same as that of his father, was near and to the north of the homestead of the late John Codman, D. D.

DESCENDANTS OF SAMUEL SPARE.

PART II.—NAMES DERIVED BY MARRIAGE.

A.

ELIZABETH[3] SPARE BRANCH.

ELIZABETH[3] SPARE (John[2], Samuel[1]) and William Fitzgerald, of Roxbury, were married by Rev. Zachariah Howard, of Canton. W. F. died Sept. 17, 1802, aged 35 years, of consumption. He was a mason, worked at his trade in Boston; resided in Canton. The couple are buried, Punkapog Cem.; marble gravestone. Their children threw off the Fitz.

    ch. i. JOHN[4], b. Feb. 9, 1794; d. July 21, 1859.
       ii. HANNAH[4], b. Oct. 18, 1795; d. Aug. 14, 1865.
      iii. JAMES[4], b. Jan. 23, 1798; d. July 23, 1880.
      iv. MARY[4], b. Nov. 19, 1800; d. May 8, 1866.

Mary was unm.; lived mostly in Boston.

JOHN[4] GERALD m., first, Dec. 31, 1817, Ruth McKendry, of Canton, who was b. July 19, 1793, and d. Jan. 6, 1839.

    ch. i. SARAH-EVERETT[5], b. Aug. 16, 1819; l.
      ii. ELIZA-ANN[5], b. Mar. 20, 1821; l.
     iii. JOHN[5], b. Sept. 12, 1825; l.
     iv. BRADFORD[5], 1st, b. July 15, 1827; d. Apr. 16, 1829.
      v. BRADFORD[5], 2d, b. Nov. 10, 1831; d. July 30, 1851.

m., second, Aug. 26, 1839, Nancy Downs, of Canton, b. July 21, 1795; d. Sept. 18, 1877. No ch.

John⁴ Gerald, was b. and spent all his life in Canton. In 1814 he was a soldier in the Canton company, drafted to go to Fort Warren, but went as a substitute for John McKendry. He was in the service two months. About 1818 he bought of Nathan Kenney (177– 1829), son of John Kenney, Esq. (1729–1805), the farm of 16 acres, next south of the 13th-milestone place. In 1827 he established the Cherry Tavern thereon, which he managed till 1842, and then resided in his house across the way till his death. Being an orphan early, he spent his boyhood with his grandfather Spare—a very industrious and determined man; recognized no obstacles in the pursuit of a plan. He dug the bog canal, 1832.

SARAH-E.⁵ GERALD m., May 18, 1843, James-Turner Sumner, who was b. Feb. 10, 1820. Reside at Canton Corner.

ch. i. SARAH-DRAPER-TURNER⁶, b. Nov. 9, 1844; l.
   ii. LARA-WENTWORTH⁶, b. Mar. 6, 1847; l.
   iii. ELIZA-ANN⁶, b. July 24, 1853; l. unm.
   iv. ALICE-MARIA⁶, b. Nov. 19, 1855; l. unm.

SARAH-DRAPER-TURNER⁶ SUMNER m., Thomas-Bailey Draper, of Canton, who was b. Melbourne, England. Reside in Canton.

ch. i. NANCY-TURNER⁷, b. Oct. 7, 1866; l.
   ii. JAMES-SUMNER⁷, b. Oct. 3, 1868; l.
   iii. ALFRED-EARNEST⁷, b.
   iv. GEORGE-THOMAS⁷, b. Sept. 12, 1873; l.
   v. EDWARD-BAILEY⁷, b. Mar. 29, 1876; l.
   vi. RUTH-MABEL⁷, b. Apr. 17, 1882; l.

LARA-WENTWORTH⁶ SUMNER m., Sept. 25, 1871, Hannah-Eliza Day. No ch. reported.

ELIZA-ANN⁵ GERALD m. Robert Bird, of Canton. He was b. Aug. 22, 1813; d. Aug. 12, 1883. R. B. was a farmer. Residence at Punkapog, where the widow remains.

ch. i. FRANK-RIPLEY⁶, b. Dec. 13, 1848; l.
   ii. ROBERT⁶, b. June 22, 1862; l. unm.

DESCENDANTS OF SAMUEL SPARE.

FRANK-R.[6] m., Sept. 22, 1880, Charlotte-Elizabeth, dau. of John Eaton, of Dedham. She b. Aug. 5, 1852; no ch. Resides at Punkapog. Shoe-leather trader in Boston.

Robert[6] is a graduate of the Canton High school.

JOHN GERALD[5], Jr., m., Nov. 29, 1855, Mary-Louisa, dau. of Enos Talbot, of Norwood. She was b. July 16, 1830. Both l. at 13th-milestone site since 1856. Farmer, and he has made the farm more productive than it was ever before.

    ch. i.   LYMAN-TALBOT[6], b. Apr. 5, 1857.
       ii.   JOHN-CURTIS[6], b. Oct. 15, 1861; l.
      iii.   FREDERIC-ENOCH[6], b. Apr. 20, 1863; l.

LYMAN-TALBOT[6] GERALD m., Dec. 3, 1882, Mary-Alice, dau. of Thomas King, of Canton; resides in Norwood.

HANNAH[4] GERALD m., . . . James McFarland; he b. in Ellsworth, Me., and d. in Boston ab. 1836-7. Killed at work at his trade as a stevedore. Resided on Bartlett street, Boston.

    ch. i.   WILLIAM[5], b. Nov. 19, 1821; l.
       ii.   CHARLES-HENRY[5], b. Feb. 12, 1823; d. Mar. , 1863, at Carney Hospital, S. Boston.
      iii.   MARY-ELLEN[5], b. ab. 1833; d. Nov. 29, 1849.

WILLIAM[5] McFARLAND m., July 23, 1843, Sarah-Rendolls Olliver, of Somerville; she b. Sept. 10, 1822.

William has been stopping for quite a while at Chicago and was there at last accounts. Has been in the theatrical business.

    ch. i. & ii.   Son[6] and daughter[6]; d. early, not named.
       iii.   JAMES-HENRY[6], b. July 30, 1846; l.

JAMES-HENRY[6] McFARLAND m., Jan. 9, 1868, Ella-Caroline Pond, who d. Aug. 16, 1874.

    ch. i.   EDITH[7], b. Oct. 20, 1868; l.

J. H. McF. has been secretary of the Mining and Stock Exchange,

Boston. He is now in the life insurance business, Devonshire street, Boston. Resides with his mother at 28 Mead street, Charlestown ; not rem. Boston P. O. Box, 2551.

JAMES[4] GERALD (Elizabeth[3] Spare, John[2], Samuel[1]) m., 1828, Emiline Ryan, of Braintree. She was b. 1811. He lived in Canton, Braintree and Randolph.

- ch. i. JAMES-WARREN[5], b. Oct. 11, 1829 ; d. ab. May 14, 1871.
- ii. GEORGE-F.[5], b. Dec. 7, 1831 ; l. unm.
- iii. WILLIAM-HENRY[5], b. Nov. 1, 1833 ; l.
- iv. JOSEPHINE[5], b. 1843 ; l.
- v. ELIZABETH-SPARE[5], b. Dec. 17, 1841 ; l.
- vi. NATHANIEL[5], b. July 21, 1846 ; l.

James-Warren m. Mary Haley ; had two ch. Parents and both ch. died several years ago.

George-F. was a soldier in the war, 1861-5, and has been in feeble health since. Resides with his mother at Randolph.

WILLIAM-HENRY[5] GERALD m. Kate Hutchins, of Edgecomb, Me.; both l. East Stoughton. He, now or lately, in the express business.

- ch. i. JENNIE[6], b. Aug. 22, 1861 ; l.
- ii. HATTIE[6], b. June 30, 1863 ; d. June 6, 1869.
- iii. NETTIE[6], b. and d. dates not certain.
- iv. NELLIE-WARREN[6], b. Nov. 3, 1872 ; l.
- v. JOSEPHINE[6], b. 1873 ; d. 1874.

JENNIE[6] GERALD m., Apr. 26, 1882, Dr. Robert T. Venemann, from Evansville, Ind. They reside in East Stoughton.

- ch. i. THEODORE-WILLIAM[7], b. Aug. 21, 1883.

JOSEPHINE[5] GERALD m. George S. Eggleston, and they live at Gibson City, Ill.

- ch. i. WARREN-NEWTON[6], b. May, 1869 ; d. Mar. 28, 1883.
- ii. MILAN-LEE[6], b. Aug. 4, 1877.
- iii. FOREST[6], b. May, 1879.
- iv. WALKER[6], b. Apr., 1883.

ELIZABETH-SPARE[5] GERALD m., Feb. 22, 1866, Newton Eggleston, and they live at 90 State street, Brooklyn, L. I. An engineer.

 ch. i. GEORGE[6], b. Oct. 11, 1867 ; l.
  ii. MYRON[6], b. Sept. 2, 1869 ; l.
  iii. FLORENCE-MABEL[6], b. Sept. 27, 1875 ; l.

NATHANIEL[5] GERALD m. Nancy Reed.

 ch. i. CLIFTON-ELLERY[6], b. May 13, 1872 ; l.
  ii. WARREN[6], b. May 14, 1875 ; l.
  iii. LESTER-REED[6], b. ab. Dec. 27, 1878 ; l.

They reside in "Waverly, Wellesly or Cochituate." Periodical dealer.

B

POLLY[3] SPARE BRANCH.

POLLY[3] SPARE (John[2], Samuel[1]) m. Theophilus Richardson, of Needham. He was b. Aug., 1779, and d. Autumn of 1812. "Baptism, 1775 May 28, a daughter of John Spare and wife named Polly."— Clark's Diary. They lived in Needham and perhaps Canton after mar.

 ch. i. MARY-ANN[4], b. Sept. 12, 1804 ; l.
  ii. MEHITABLE[4], b. . . . , 1806 ; d. . . . , 1806, two or three days old.
  iii. AARON[4], b. July 22, 1808 ; d. Oct. 15, 1877.
  iv. ELBRIDGE[4], b. . . . ; d. "young."

MARY-ANN[4] RICHARDSON m., May 14, 1834, Caleb Craft, of Brookline. He was b. May 19, 1805 ; d. July 30, 1875.

 ch. i. ELIZABETH[5], b. Oct. 28, 1835 ; d. Sept. 22, 1856.
  ii. JOHN-NEWTON[5], b. Mar. 6, 1838 ; d. Oct. 13, 1855.
  iii. CALEB-FRANCIS[5], b. June 21, 1842 ; d. Jan. 12, 1845.

Mrs. M. A. Craft lives in Needham, having adopted a grand-nephew as son.* In her young days she lived in Canton, John Davenport's

---

* See next page.

family, some years, but resided in Brookline after marriage and while her husband lived.

AARON[4] RICHARDSON m., Mar. 9, 1834, Sally Vose. She was b. Apr. 14, 1812; d. June 28, 1865. Before marriage he lived with "Uncle Elijah" and with Abel Wentworth, of Canton. Learned shoemaking, which he worked at more than 40 years at Stoughton.

- ch. i. FRANCIS-ADELBERT[5], b. Aug. 27, 1835; d. Mar. 15, 1871.
- ii. JAMES-WALLACE[5], b. May 1, 1837; l. m.
- iii. GILBERT-ROSHVILLE[5], b. Oct. 18, 1839; unm.; d. Feb. 18, 1869.
- iv. SARAH-ELIZABETH[5], b. Sept. 26, 1841; m.; d. Dec. 1, 1872.
- v. LUCY-ESTEN[5], b. Mar. 7, 1847; m.; d. Nov. 25, 1872.
- vi. MARY-ANNA[5], b. Sept. 2, 1850; l. m.
- vii. MARTHA-ELLEN[5], b. Apr. 29, 1853; l. m.

FRANCIS-ADELBERT[5] RICHARDSON m., Nov. 3, 1858, Sophronia B. Kimball. She is living in Stoughton.

- ch. i. ARTHUR-ADELBERT[6], b. Dec. 2, 1860; l.
- ii. FRANCIS-ROSHVILLE[6], b. Jan. 26, 1865; l.

F. R. has been adopted by his great-aunt Craft, his name changed to Caleb-Francis Craft, and lives in Needham.

- iii. JENNIE[6], b. Nov. 13, 1868; l.

JAMES-WALLACE[5] RICHARDSON m., Jan. 13, 1861, Augusta Faxon. Lives in Stoughton; in the provision business.

- ch. i. MABEL-AUGUSTA[6], b. Jan. 7, 1862; l.
- ii. EDITH-EMILY[6], b. Oct. 28, 1863; d. Aug. 22, 1866.
- iii. BERTHA-AMANDA[6], b. Feb. 3, 1868; l.
- iv. SALLY-VOSE[6], }
- v. HARRIET-HOYT[6], } b. June 8, 1872; l.

SARAH-ELIZABETH[5] RICHARDSON m., Jan. 1, 1859, James

S. Hayward. He was a private in Co. I, 12 Mass. Vol. Militia. KILLED AT THE BATTLE OF ANTIETAM, Sept. 17, 1862, aged 37 years 7 months 11 days. He was b. in Mansfield.

    ch. i. JAMES-FRANCIS[6], b. Nov. 1, 1859 ; d. Nov.   , 1859.
       ii. ELBRIDGE-AARON[6], b. Nov. 26, 1860 ; l.

LUCY-ESTEN[5] RICHARDSON m., Sept., 1866, George-Warren Smith.

    ch. i. LEONE-FRANCIS[6], b. Apr. 11, 1867 ; l.
      ii. GILBERT-RICHARDSON[6], b. Feb. 18, 1869 ; d. same day.

Residence, Stoughton.

MARY-ANNA[5] RICHARDSON m., May 20, 1875, Henry Gardner Burrel, of Stoughton ; no ch. reported. Both living in Stoughton.

MARTHA-ELLEN[5] RICHARDSON m., Nov. 4, 1876, Henry-Everett French, of Easton, and there reside.

    ch. i. ELLA[6], b. Aug. 24, 1877, in California.
      ii. ANNA-AUGUSTA[6], b. July 15, 1879 ; l.

C

JAMES[3] SPARE BRANCH.

ELIZA[4] SPARE (James[3], John[2], Samuel[1]) m., ab. 1845, Samuel Bowden, then of Boston, where he had been a policeman. He was from Kennebunk, Me. He died of Bright's disease, Jan., 1868; kept house in North Bennet street. No ch., but had adopted Bessie ———, who m. Wesley Cutting ; moved with their mother to Milwaukee, where they are now living (1879). Eliza d. there and was buried at Hopkinton, Mass. Before marriage E. had been a tailoress many years in Boston.

HARRIET[4] SPARE (James[3], John[2], Samuel[1]) mar. Amos Esty. She had lived in a family at Scot's Wood, then at Benjamin McKendry's toll-house, Milton, afterward at Amory's till married. She and husband celebrated their golden wedding May 2, 1880, and both are now living at Oak Hill, Newton ; West Roxbury P. O. He and son are market-garden producers. H. S. and A. E. were m. May 2, 1830, in Milton.

    ch. i. CHARLES[5], b. May 16, 1834 ; l. m.
        ii. AMOS[5],   } b. Feb., 1839 ; "lived five weeks."
       iii. ARTEMAS[5], } b. Feb., 1839 ; d. Sept. 15, 1861.

CHARLES[5] ESTY m., Apr. 27, 1863, Emiline Clements, of Berwick Great Falls, Me.

    ch. i. HERMAN-CLEMENT[6], b. Oct. 3, 1866 ; l.
        ii. FREDERIC-SPARE[6], b. Oct. 27, 1870; l.
       iii. JAMES-PAYSON[6], b. Aug. 1, 1874 ; l.

ABIGAIL-CRANE[5] SPARE (James[4], James[3], John[2], Samuel[1]) m., Dec. 3, 1855, Darius R. Mead. He was b. in Meadville, Pa., Dec. 23, 1832, and d. Feb. 19, 1878. Mrs. A. C. M. and children are living at Rockford, Ill. He was a lumber dealer.

    ch. i. FRANK-WILSON[6], b. Sept. 21, 1856 ; l.
        ii. HATTIE-L.[6], b. Nov. 29, 1859 , l.
       iii. RUTH-TITCOMB[6], b. July 6, 1862 ; l.
       iv. MINNIE-SPARE[6], b. Oct. 13, 1863 ; d. Oct. 6, 1869.
        v. MARY-IDALETTE[6], b. Mar. 15, 1866 ; l.
       vi. DURAND-RAY[6], } b. Dec. 6, 1868.
      vii. GERTRUDE[6], }
     viii. GEORGE-WASHINGTON[6], b. Feb. 22, 1871.
       ix. WALTER-SPARE[6], b. Dec. 17, 1874.

FRANK-WILSON[6] Mead m., Oct. 6, 1880, Motte Gibbons.

    ch. i. ROYAL-JAY[7], b. July 22, 1881.

ELIZA-TITCOMB[5] SPARE (James[4], James[3], John[2], Samuel[1]) m., Apr. 16, 1868, Rev. David W. Evans, who was b. in Wales, G. B. He graduated at Beloit College, Wis, 1862 ; Union Theo. Sem., N. Y.,

DESCENDANTS OF SAMUEL SPARE. 43

1863. His first charge was at Sauk Centre, Minn.; then at Rushville, Ill., nine years. He contributed to Norton's History of Presbyterianism in Southern Illinois. He d. Dec. 10, 1881. Widow and ch. r. in Rockford, Ill.

    ch. i. HOBART-JAMES^6, b. Dec. 27, 1869 ; l.
       ii. MARY-BELLE^6, b. Oct. 12, 1871 ; l.
      iii. RUTH-CAROLINE^6, b. Nov. 27, 1873 ; l.
      iv. PAUL-LEWELLYN^6, b. Aug. 23, 1876 ; l.
       v. DAVID-SUMNER^6, b. Dec. 27, 1880 ; l.

SARAH-LAMBERT^5 SPARE (James^4, James^3, John^2, Samuel^1) m., June 4, 1868, William C. Murtfeldt, who was b. Apr. 2, 1844, and is l. at Rockford, Ill.; farmer.

    ch. i. FREDERIC-JAMES^6, b. Nov. 13, 1870.
       ii. MINNIE-AUGUSTA^6, b. June 23, 1872.
      iii. CHARLES-SPARE^6, b. Jan. 9, 1874 ; d. Apr. 3, 1880.

CECELIA-KENT^5 SPARE (Bayard^4, James^3, John^2, Samuel^1) m., Aug. 2, 1867, Charles A. Sanborn. They l. at North Beverly, Mass.

    ch. i. MARCIA-FRANCES^6, b. Dec. 15, 1872 ; d. Mar. 14, 1875.

MARY-FRANCES^5 (Bayard^4, James^3, John^2, Samuel^1) m., Sept. 28, 1871, Daniel-Albert Kingsbury ; r. East Boston ; street railroad business.

    ch. i. MARY-ELLA^6, b. Dec. 14, 1872 ; l.
       ii. WILLIAM-BAYARD^6, b. Mar. 23, 1874 ; d. May 9, 1876.
      iii. DANIEL-WALTER^6, b. June 16, 1877 ; d. Apr. 28, 1878.

SARAH-CROWE^4 SPARE (James^3, John^2, Samuel^1) m., Mar. 13, 1834, Daniel Stevens, of Bridgeport, N. J. He d. Apr. 10, 1883.

    ch. i. MARY-JANE^5, b. Jan. 14, 1835; d. Oct. 9, 1873 ; m.
       ii. ANN-ELIZA^5, b. June 3, 1836 ; l. m.

DESCENDANTS OF SAMUEL SPARE.

 iii. EDWARD[5], b. Aug. 30, 1838 ; d. Sept., 1839.
 iv. MARGARET-ELMER[5], b. Oct. 3, 1840 ; unm.; l. at Odessa, Del.
 v. AMANDA-SPARE[5], b. Mar. 26, 1843 ; d. Nov. 30, 1858.
 iv. EDMOND-SAMUEL[5], b. June 10, 1845.
 vii. EMMA-FRANCES[5], b. Dec. 12, 1847 ; d. Feb. 10, 1852.
 viii. ALFRED[5], } b. Feb. 7, 1850 ; l. m.
 ix. WILLIAM[5], } b. Feb. 7, 1850 ; d. at birth.
 x. CECELIA[5], b. Apr. 30, 1852 ; d. May 2, 1852.

MARY-JANE[5] STEVENS m., May 27, 1855, Robert Swan ; l. at Odessa, Del.

 ch. i. ALONZO[6], b. Mar. 4, 1855 ; l.
 ii. DANIEL[6], b. Apr. 24, 1856 ; d. June 18, 1858.
 iii. EMMA-JANE[6], b. July 9, 1859 ; l.
 iv. IDA-SPARE[6], b. Oct. 9, 1860 ; l.
 v. GEORGE-SAMUEL[6], b. Dec. 1, 1862 ; l.
 vi. ALFRED-F.[6], b. June 12, 1864 ; l.
 vii. JOHN[6], b. May 27, 1866 ; l.
 viii. WILLIAM-MARSHAL[6], b. Nov. 27, 1868 ; l.
 ix. DANIEL-STEVENS[6], b. Jan. 17, 1873 ; l.

ANN-ELIZA[5] STEVENS m., Jan. 4, 1857, Thomas Davis, of Baltimore. Both l. in Baltimore.

 ch. i. ELLA[6], b. Feb. 2, 1859 ; l. (1879).
 ii. AMANDA-E.[6], b. Dec. 9, 1861 ; l.
 iii. AMY-BELLE[6], b. Nov. 17, 1865 ; l.

EDMOND-SAMUEL[5] STEVENS m., Feb. 23, 1871, Lizzie Evans.

 ch. i. OLIVER[6], b. Nov. 19, 1871.
 ii. WALTER-EVANS[6], b. June 23, 1873 ; d. Nov. 8, 1873.
 iii. HARRY[6], b. Mar. 2, 1875 ; d. Oct. 7, 1877.

ALFRED[5] STEVENS m., Apr. 27, 1875, Eliza Moody. These and ch. are living (1879) at

 ch. i. HELEN[6], b. Feb. 12, 1876,
 ii. BERTHA[6], b. Feb. 27, 1877.
 iii. STANLEY[6], b. Mar. 6, 1878.

DESCENDANTS OF SAMUEL SPARE.

ELIZABETH[5], (Francis-Waite[4] Spare, James[3], John[2], Samuel[1]) m., 1864, George Skaith, a native of England. Live in Tabor, Fremont Co., Iowa.

    ch. i. JOHN-FRANCIS[6], b. Mar. 2, 1865.
      ii. MARY-MARTHA[6], b. Dec. 6, 1867.
      iii. GEORGE[6], b. May 17, 1869.
      iv. JAMES-EDWARD[6], b. Dec. 12, 1870; d. Apr. 12, 1871.
      v. SARAH-ANN[6], b. Mar. 21, 1872.
      vi. EFFIE[6], b. Mar. 8, 1875.
      vii. WILLIAM[6], b. May 2, 1877.
      viii. ROBERT[6], b. Oct. 21, 1879.
      ix. ROYE[6], b. Sept. 27, 1881.

MARGARET[5] (Francis-Waite[4], James[3], John[2], Samuel[1]) m., Nov. 2, 1867, William Marshall; live in Tabor, Fremont Co., Iowa.

    ch. i. JOHN-FRANCIS[6], b. Aug. 1, 1868.
      ii. SARAH-ANN[6], b. Sept. 1, 1870.
      iii. WILLIAM[6], b. Apr. 6, 1873.

CAROLINE[4] SPARE (James[3], John[2], Samuel[1]) m., June 20, 1851, Jacob Raymond; he d. after 1879. He had been keeper of the Delaware House at Smyrna, Del. Children living, 1879.

    ch. i. MARY[5], b. Apr. 14, 1852.
      ii. GEORGE-H.[5], b. Nov. 10, 1854.
      iii. JACOB[5], b. Dec. 12, 1856.

MEHITABLE[3] SPARE BRANCH.

MEHITABLE[3] SPARE (John[2], Samuel[1]) m., first, Aug. 21, 1800, John Parmer, by John Lathrop, all of Boston. He died at sea, when his son Granville "was very young," say 1815; lived in Boston. His grand-children spell it Palmer.

    ch. i. GRANVILLE[4], b. Jan. 2, 1812; d. Sept. 20, 1882, at Cambridge.

M. P. m., second, ab. 1817, John Eastrom (Eastern, ? Restrum, ?) who d. in freezing weather ab. 1822-3 and was b. under St. Matthew's Church, South Boston. It was icy at the time ; the bearers slipped and dropped the body—an incident of peculiar remembrance. Lived in Boston.

 ch. ii. ELIZABETH[4], b. ab. 1818, and d. "many years ago." She m.   Dam, and is supposed by the widow of Granville to have issue living. Special letters for information failed of results.

  iii. ANDREW[4], b. ab. 1821. The last gathered about him is that he was a boy in an asylum.

  iv. JOHN[4], b. after 1821 ; nothing further known.

  v.? One child died in Canton in Feb., 1824. It is not known whether this was John or another.

GRANVILLE[4] PARMER m.,   Harriet Colson, then of Canton, but was from "down East." She is l. at 111½ Inman street, Cambridgeport.

 ch. i. MALVINA[5] PALMER, b. 183– ; d. at the age of 22 years 3 months, "twenty or more years ago" ; unm.

  ii. ORLANDO[5] M. PALMER, b. Nov. 27, 1841.

  iii. GEORGIE-ANNA[5], b. . . . ; l. m.

ORLANDO[5] m., . . ., Louisa-Josephine Ryder. They reside in Linden (Malden), with two children or more, names not ascertained. He is in the provision business.

GEORGIE-A.[5] m., ab. 1876, William Johnson, and they are living in Cambridge.

 ch. i. SUMNER[6], b. ab. 1878.

Granville learned the carpenter's trade of Wm. McKendry, of Punkapog, and while with him the writer saw him at work in 1829, reseating the school-house there, at its entirely-new reconstruction. He lived in

DESCENDANTS OF SAMUEL SPARE. 47

Cambridge many years at this business, with residence at 19 Bigelow street. Born in Boston, but spent some of his boyhood and youth in Canton; was perhaps a year at uncle Elijah's. Some amusing anecdotes omitted. Orlando M. resembles him very remarkably.

E

PEGGY[3] SPARE BRANCH.

PEGGY[3] SPARE (John[2], Samuel[1]), b. in Canton, went to Boston young; m., ab. 1817, Peter Wilson, a native of Sweden, who came to America ab. 1816. He was b. Dec. 13, 1779, and d. Jan. 24, 1864. The couple lived in Boston (at one time on Lovell's Island) till 1824; then in Canton till 1833; then in Boston till death. He and his brother once owned and ran a schooner. He had been in the British naval service, and saw Napoleon Bonaparte when he was taken on board the Northumberland. So he told the writer.

    ch. i. JAMES-LORENZO[4], b. June 10, 1819; d. Feb. 20, 1883.
        ii. JOHN[4], b. Jan. 28, 1821; d. Sept. 21, 1821.
       iii. MARY-NELSON[4], b. Mar. 8, 1823; l. in Boston.
       iv. HARRIET[4], b. July 14, 1828; d. Oct. 4, 1833; b. Canton; d. Boston.

JAMES-L.[4] m., April 26, 1848, Frances-Rebecca, dau. of Robert S. Blake, of Boston. She was b. and is living in Boston.

    ch. Two twin daughters, b. Spring of 1852; l. two days; unnamed.

James-L.[4] learned the printer's art; was foreman with Eastman six years, who left him a small legacy as a testimonial to his worth and reliableness. He was then, for more than 20 years, with Rand & Avery, whom he left by reason of the failing of his health, about three years before his death of consumption. He was buried in the Cambridge Cemetery. His obituary in the *Daily Advertiser* is by A. C. R., for 25 years an intimate friend.

R. S. B. was well acquainted with John[2] Spare. He put the first paint on the then new State House in 1800.

F

ELIJAH[3] SPARE BRANCH.

SARAH-ELIZABETH[5] SPARE, dau. of Elijah[4], m., Nov. 13, 1864, John-Murray Hastings, of East Cambridge. Both are living. He is in the glass business there.

ch. i. NELLIE-EVERET[6], b. Apr. 25, 1867; l.

ANTOINETTE[5] SPARE, dau. of Elijah[4], m., Nov. 13, 1868 or 9, Charles Bent, of Cambridge. They resided on Charles River street. He is connected with the Riverside Press.

ch. i CHARLES-LYMAN[6], b. ab. 1871; l.
ii. } Twin daughters, b. . . . ; one lived six weeks the other
iii. } seven months.

NANCY-C.[4] SPARE (Elijah[3], John[2], Samuel[1]) m., July 7, 1847, Elisha Locke, from Durham or New Durham, N. H. She had attended the Middleboro Academy, was a fine scholar and much beloved. The couple went immediately after marriage to Cincinnati, O., and settled, he to teach music. The cholera was prevalent at Cincinnati and she was taken with it, bringing on premature childbirth, and, as the dates show, her death in three days.* Her ambrotype, now with the writer, is a source of saddened recollections.

He is still living at Clifton Heights, Cincinnati, Dec., 1883; rem.,

---

* Page 29.

DESCENDANTS OF SAMUEL SPARE. 49

and with children. He spent the years 1839-40 in Canton, where he taught the district school one winter.

 ch. i. ALMIRA⁵, ⎫ b. July 10, 1849 ; one lived one, the
  ii. LOUISA-MARIA⁵, ⎬ other three weeks.

SARAH-JANE⁴ SPARE (Elijah³, John², Samuel¹) m., Mar. 23, 1870, Albert-Atwood Rotch, Esq., of Easton. They resided in an eligible residence cor. of Bay and William streets, Easton. The sufferings of the last year of her life, afflicted with a dreadful case of Bright's disease with continued confinement to bed, she bore with unexampled endurance. Buried with her husband at Furnace Cemetery, Easton. Reads her head-stone :

  "Her virtues will embalm her memory,"

A. A. R. was b. in Boston, July, 1810, and d. May 21, 1883 He was acquainted with the art of moulding and casting iron, and of thread manufacture ; had been leader of a musical band and of a church choir : surveyed land ; was an amateur printer ; held various town offices ; had been trial justice ; assessor of internal revenue. S. J. S. was his second wife. These had no children.

ELIZABETH-BARBER⁴ SPARE (Elijah³, John², Samuel¹) m., Nov. 24, 1842, Clifford Belcher, Jr., of Canton. She died of consumption, lingering about seven years, for the last three of which she did not leave the house, nor for the last two scarcely her bed. She had many sympathizing and kind friends who were unwearied in their devotion to her comfort. Buried in Canton Central Cemetery, north extremity. He was b. Apr. 29, 1821, and is l., and rem. to Arvilla Dean, of Easton. Residence, Walnut street, Canton.

 ch. i. FREDERIC-CLIFFORD⁵, b. Nov. 7, 1844 ; l.
  ii. CHARLES-EDWIN⁵, b. Jan. 5, 1848 ; l.
  iii. ADELAIDE-LOUISA⁵, b. Oct. 13, 1850 ; l. unm.
  iv. ELMER-AUGUSTINE⁵, b. Apr. 25, 1853 ; d. Oct. 18, 1883.

FREDERIC-CLIFFORD⁵ BELCHER m. Mary Drake, dau. of Andrew Drake, of Canton. She d. Jan. 17, 1870 ; no ch. He is l., not rem. ; a machinist.

CHARLES-EDWIN[5] BELCHER m., Nov. 21, 1872, Eleanor McGlathlin, of Chelsea. Both are l. in Canton.

    ch. i. WALTER[6], b. Aug. 31, 1873; l.
       ii. STELLA-ADELAIDE[6], b. Mar. 31, 1881; l.

Adelaide[5]-L. is a graduate of the Canton High school.

ELMER-AUGUSTINE[5] m., June 9, 1879, Frances-Waltena, dau. of Walter Dean, of Canton. Lived in Canton and Brockton.

    ch. i. HELEN-ELIZABETH[6], b. Mar. 17, 1882; l.

CHRIST CHURCH, SALEM STREET.

SOME REMARKS ADDITIONAL.

(*EXPLANATORY AND CORRECTIVE.*)

We have arrived at the end of our genealogy; it is as complete as it could be made, except by delay, and even expense and travel to gain the very few missing dates.

The genealogical record presents a sad number of early deaths—of infants, of youths, of persons dying in early manhood and womanhood, and in middle adult life—a greater proportion than is usual in most families. One utility of such a record is the setting before the survivors and the coming generations the lesson : Take care.

The twins are several times more numerous than is usual with a like number of births in the whole community, and with what early fatality !

The pages being fewer than had been anticipated, a few matters may be here touched again, which were already possessed or have since been gathered, and we have engravings to offer which were not at the beginning of the printing supposed to be so feasible.

Obligations should be expressed to DANIEL V. T. HUNTOON, Esq., of Canton, who, although he did not labor expressly for this work, had, by his publications and personal correspondence with the writer, made accessible matters relating to the English church of Canton, especially the relations of the Spare family to it and the names of the communicants, which the writer had in former years supposed irrevocably lost, and most of the old papers from the town archives.

Obligations are also due to John C. Spare, James W. Richardson,

James H. McFarland and Robert Bird, Jr., for their very complete and perfect returns.

On the title page the word *compiled* might as well not be there, as the matter has been obtained at first sources.

"Our oxen," page 15, should be understood to be the oxen of Spare's and Tilson's own team.

On page 16 read : Samuel, aged 14 years 7 months, etc.

On page 24 for McCormack read McCormick.

On page 31 read Forest Hills.

On page 37 read Oliver—one l.

On page 20 the word excommunicated is used facetiously but unfortunately. In fact and by ecclesiastical law, John Spare appointed warden (not for the first time) on June 11, 1776, held that office 44 years till his death. Since the assembling of the church communicants, omitted for sufficient reasons, affects the standing of no one of them in the comprehensive and still existing church.

In the terrible excitements of that month, the church, at its meeting on that day felt the hour upon them, for a postponement of meeting, till a new notice; it never came, but this was not foreseen.

For readers at a distance, let it be said that on June 11, 1876, a Memorial Meeting was held in the church nearest the site of the English church—the church of the First Congregational Society—designed to call up and impress on the present generation the Canton English Church, practically extinct as to holding services for a century. Mr. Huntoon gave a historical address. Descendants of old communicants were present who lived one hundred miles apart. There were responsive readings from the prayer-book, special rendering of music by an enlarged choir and elaborate floral decorations. And will it be believed, Richard Clark, son of Reverend Wm. Clark, was present, induced to sit in the pulpit, at the age of 79, coming from Boston; and a painted portrait of that father, the last rector.

THE SALTER–KENNEY HOUSE.—Charles Salter, of Boston, bought the land here, 60 acres, of William Bennett in 1700, having no buildings thereon. He was a carpenter and must have built at once. His widow sold this place to Jonathan Kenney (1670–1722) in the year 1714. The committee appointed by the town of Dorchester in 1700 to lay out the highway between Milton line and Mr. Billings, in Sharon, "began

House of SAMUEL SPARE 1730-1856

at Milton line and so marked the way as followeth × × × × next a gray oak tree against Mr. Salter's door on the west side of the way × × ×."*

This was probably the third house built for English settlers for the present territory of Canton, Stoughton, Sharon, Foxboro and Wrentham. One of the others was Matthias Puffer's, in 1691, on cor. of Blue Hill and Washington streets; the remaining one, Billing's tavern, in Sharon— the second house as respects Canton.

The present Davenport house, on the Puffer site, is an old one and is the third one thereon.

The first sermon ever preached in the above territory to the English settlers was in the Salter house. This tradition has come down to the writer through his mother and grandfather and its carrying by them covers three-fourths of the period. Mr. Huntoon, who admits the correctness of the tradition, thinks Rev. Oxenbridge Thatcher, of Milton, was the preacher.

It was in this house that Samuel Spare must have lived three months in 1738, for John Keny owned it, his mother having then probably died, and John had another house, the one next to the north on the land of the same purchase; or rather of an additional purchase at another date, wherein he was living, having married Elizabeth Wentworth, in 1728.

The 13th-milestone Spare house on old Salter-Kenney site, occupies a commanding site, about half a mile south of Blue Hill; from its rear the sight overlooks Dedham, Norwood, and perhaps Dover, and discovers Wachuset Mountain, 50 miles away. For 49 years the rumbling of the cars of the Boston & Providence railroad, many times a day, as they pass over Fowl Meadows at the west, have been there heard.

One Kenney house at the north, and two Kenney houses next to it at the south, at one time contained neighbors of that name, while others still of the name were on Green Lodge street. The writer puts it on record here that he has collected in manuscript a full genealogy of this Canton family of Kenneys from 1670 to 1833, when as a name it became extinct in the town, and has identified nine house sites.

Each of these three houses (the Spare house *was* one) had near them, when the writer was young, large and valuable cherry trees, such as are now never seen, and they gave a distinction to the locality for that reason.

We give a photo-engraving of the house; the barn was built in 1827. The old one, a century old, on a different site, was removed to a more western site to be used for a cider mill, and went to decay after 1845.

---

* From their report to the town.

CHRIST CHURCH is the oldest church edifice in Boston. On the ground it is 60 feet long by 45 feet wide; it has side galleries; the windows have small, diamond-shaped panes; the church has a tower which supports a spire 175 feet high, "it being one of the most elegant steeples in the United States."* The central aisle, originally present, had then, 1817, been removed "within a few years and its place occupied with pews," but of the old construction, with straight-up, high backs and equally high doors to the pews. On the frieze is inscribed: "This is none other than the House of God and this is the gate of Heaven." The church has a chime of eight bells. Their respective weights and the contributors' names are in Antique Views of Boston.

LAMB TAVERN.—From the Barber inventory:

"Goods and chattels,	£1490
Sundries in cash collected,	95 18
There is also in Real Estate,	1322
Old Tenor,	2907 18
Debts and Expenses,	674 3
[Net Estate]	2233 15"

The debts paid are in 47 items, among which were "gloves for the funeral, £10; mourning, £30" If there had been a mortgage on real estate it must have been included and paid by "debts." There was no will, because Eunice *Leonard* was administratrix. Supposing that one per cent. of the value of the Dorchester estate should be represented by the town rates, page 18, we should have its value, £225. Using £225 as sufficiently reliable, we have the value of the real estate of the Lamb Tavern site (1322—225) £1097, or, reduced to silver dollars (of one ounce each, at the value of old Tenor paper, 28s. the ounce at that time), 627 dollars. But silver in 1744 would purchase four or five times as much of corn or labor as now. This lifts the value back again. But the heart of Boston, with 140 years' more growth is the other factor, and the writer leaves the subject to the imagination.

Our picture shows the Tavern, a wooden building, as it was in 1833 when the writer boarded therein, and as it had been, with its sign of the Lamb projecting over Washington street, certainly since 1746.

Before he was "inholder," Hezekiah Barber had been a blacksmith.

---

* *Shaw's History of Boston.*—1817.

3ᵈ Spare House 1777-1855 Now J Gerald's, Canton

DESCENDANTS OF SAMUEL SPARE.

James Leonard, the husband and new *incumbent*, had been one of Barber's employés. He had the inside track. It would seem from the early marriage that "the funeral baked meats did serve the marriage feast" Her name was Leonard before the estate was settled.

While this sheet is being put in type, a search for Hezekiah Barber's gravestone has not been successful. Other stones, his father's and mother's (James and Elizabeth), and the others following, are in Dorchester Old Cemetery, closely contiguous to the walled corner of Boston and Stoughton streets.

> Here Lyes ye Body of Mr James Barber. He died Oct 13 1732 aged About 80^{ty} years.
>
> Here Lyes ye Body of Mrs Elizabeth Barber Widow of Mr James Barber She dec^d ye 4th of Decr 1739 in ye 81st year of her age.
>
> Jesse Barber Son to Hezekiah & Eunice Barber. He died May ye 2^d 1734 in ye 10 year of his age.
>
> Lois Barber Daughter to Mr Hezekiah & Mrs Eunice Barber died Sept ye 2^d 1739 aged 2 ye^s & 4 da^s.
>
> Grace Barber Daugh^r to Mr Hezekiah & Mrs Eunice Barber died Decr 1st 1740 aged 1 year 2 mo^s & 17 days.
>
> Sarah Barber Daughter to John & Mary Barber died 18th Sept 1735 aged 12 days.
>
> Sarah Barber ye Daughter of John & Mary Barber died April ye 26 1739 aged 1 week & 4 days.

The date of James Barber's death, given on page 34, although correctly transcribed from the old copy of Saint's Everlasting Rest, with the word "about." must give way to the gravestone; it was as near as the recorder knew.

This same book, preserved by Abigail C. Mead, contains an old entry that Samuel Spare was of Devonshire Co., England, confirming the tradition given on page 4.

Hezekiah Barber's daughters, one or more, or their next generation, marrying, gave rise to the names Wilcox, Willis and Rice; persons of these names in Boston were often mentioned by the writer's father as somehow related, and he kept up their acquaintance. Also with Mrs. Mary Barnard Dolliver; this was certainly her name, though unintentionally omitted on page 22. It was possibly too much of a hazard to give *Mary-Barnard* Emerson as the name of her mother.

62   DESCENDANTS OF SAMUEL SPARE.

The following lines were written Centennial year. Canton is a town full of historical incidents, reaching back to 1650 or 1657, in which latter year the Punkapog Indians were located here, as wards of the State. Blue Hill, 712 feet above tide water, is its most distinguishing physical feature. Some of the old Indian chiefs had their headquarters near it—*on it,* says Shaw's History of Boston. From the Indian name of the hill the name Massachusetts is derived. The lines hit on many of the historical points, and all are authentic, uttered a little elevated and loud, as they needed to be, the hill is so high. Seven generations of the stock whose record this book gives, have gazed upon it and ascended it, if the youngest have been old enough to do so.

T. D. J., grandson of the Colonel who was born in the now-standing Col. Doty Inn, and who, remembered by the writer, died about 1825, in early middle age, was the hero of the rock exploit. He was about six feet and a half high, and relatively large and broad-shouldered. He used to amaze the crowd with feats of strength, and had done this in the streets of Boston. My aged informant remembered the rock affair and also the wood-chute. The writer remembers "Doty-des," and has been with boys who tried the same play in a necessarily small way.

This hill was illuminated on the repeal of the Stamp Act by the British Parliament; on the promulgation of the Declaration of Independence, and on the surrenders of Burgoyne and Cornwallis. The sentinels were there all during the British occupation of Boston, with torch ready to light signal fires at any moment. So spake William Dunbar, Esq., in an oration delivered from the highest platform of its Observatory, July 4, 1826, saying also: "This mountain is therefore consecrate and hallowed ground, *dedicated to Liberty and Independence.*"

CENTENNIAL WORDS WITH BLUE HILL.

Mound first to greet the inbound sailor's eye
    Of all the Bay State raises to the sky,
    Blue Hill! the chief of Granite Quarry Range
    Whence builders hewed for Boston her Exchange,
    A solid seat of Customs pillared strange,
    And Shaft,—The rocks shall raise their head
    Of his deeds to tell—so WARREN said;
    Thy front close viewed through all my youthful days
    From window pane, from school, from works and plays,
    'Tis Eighteen Seventy-six! I give to thee salute,
    Centennial year! O Hill of wide repute.

Solid and massive, thy stern and craggy form
    Defies the fierceness of the raging storm;
    Feels not within a stroke or piercing bore
    By dynamite for iron track or ore;

No herds or flocks without of grazing brute
Thy mossy rocks or scanty grass dispute;
Thy face and eyes turn noonward bare and quick,
Thy flanks and rear wear forests rank and thick,
They doff this coat when eager axes click,
Down the swift wood-chute, on a headlong course,
Oak chases ash, beech birch, excusing horse.
By carts to town, by armfuls to the hearth,
The cuts aflame, they crackle out in worth;
The folks there circled taste the sweets of earth.

Thy brow's a precipice, scarce a path allowed;
Rough rocks they cluster, scraggy shrubs they crowd;
MEDUSA, has she lent her horrid hairs!
For serpents dire curl rank about thy ears!
Lurk mid the vines and Berries of the Bears!
The traveler shudders at that larum trill!
And flees for life or fights resolved to kill!

Escaped the venom and the deadly bite,
I mount and view the grand out-reaching sight.
A temple's dome! — The arching is the sky,
Thou art the altar built up heavenly high;
There the cloud curtains kept in place by winds,
While all below is pavement, and its tile designs
Are seas and townships and the forest pines.
This mirror-pond, all skirted with a grove,
Paints it with boughs adown, and trunks above,
Tile Boston reaches to Neponset's tide,
Her dome and spires, her Bunker shaft espied;
Dorchester reads like checkered story ground,
And Milton writ on Paradise Refound!
At dawn in Quincy, presidential soil,
Hear clinking drills rehearse her flinty toil;
At noon in Stoughton's "land beyond Blue Hills,"
Her sutor-craft swift whirled by vapor mills;
Judicial Dedham woos the setting sun;
A hundred townships tiled the pave is done,
Seen through the depths of misty haze,
All round when wheeled the telescopic gaze.

O, born of Earth, of Adamantine germ,
    Torpid, hirsute and massive pachyderm!
    Had mother groaning with intestine pains
    Tumultuous, shook thee with convulsive strains;
    Or why came tumbling from thy bosom down,
    Thy diamond, a terror to the town?
    Is grinding in the furious manner done
    The best of ways to polish precious stone?

"Some human wags pried off a balanced rock,
    It whirled and thundered with terrific shock;
    Great oaks were rended by the restless mass,
    Nor stopped it till it blocked the public pass;
    Long drilled and split, the meteor gave the way;
    Ajax DOTYDES led that sportive day,
    That vexed all Canton with a tax to pay."

I need not ask thee all about thy birth,
    What posed thee so upon the mother Earth,
    What Fates were thine through æons that are past
    Melted and cooled, or crystalized and cast;
    How glaciers scored thee freighting bowlders by
    And piled with drift thy northern slope so high;
    But yester- and to-day, relate, O Hill.

"I saw the Mayflower moored in winter chill,
    The Pilgrim land and build his frail abode,
    The Colony expand, the forest mowed;
    The Province of the Massachusetts Bay
    Lay out her towns beneath the royal sway;
    The dusky native's dart within my gaze,
    Struck the wild deer,—the soil gave only maize.
    As midst Mars Hill the Apostle did exhort,
    So midst Blue Hill has Eliot prayed and taught.
    He 'gospelizing' Second Praying Town,
    Near this bright Pond preached Punkapog's renown,
    Men of New Athens glimpsed the Great Unknown.

When Philip raged with tomahawk and brand,
    The sentry paced me firelock in hand,—

When George sent hirelings to repress our cause,
The sentry walked me, he that knows no pause."

Now comes a third centennial mark—a Show—
At Brother Love, where Schuylkill waters flow,
No sentry paces now his weary tread.
Where spears spread want, the reaper's hook gives bread.

Here at thy feet does Doty's Inn abide,
Relate the tale why hither WARREN'S ride?

"Ere yet the corn of 'Seventy-Four was brown
First Suffolk Congress vowed against the Crown—
We'll pay no tribute used to tramp us down—
And quaffed the spring at DOTY'S on this plain,
My mountain mass distilled from crystal rain."

What warrior-guest within its gambrel nook
Its simple fare and cooling goblet took,
And sought in sleep to drown his weary throes?

"My boughs and breeze fanned LAFAYETTE'S repose.
Across the way proud Royall tilled the soil,
That open plain, with Afric's sable toil;
His right arm prayed from Britain to be loose,
His left shipped slaves to Antigua for use!
Next roof young BUSSEY smote the silver ore,
His school was one, his home three furlongs more;
The same for HARVARD planted Farmer's Lore.
That foundry fumes near PAUL REVERE'S abode,
His steed struck fire upon the midnight road,
While inland the invading British strode.
His neighbor GRIDLEY bled on Bunker's field;
He planned the trench his comrades' breasts to shield,
But bared his own with only courage steeled.

There SHERMAN lived, the Land Declared he Free,
His Life and Luck and Honor pledging he;
There DOWNS, the hero of Quallah Battoo,—
His Naval story tells the praises due;
There Sassamon's birth, he was King Philip's scribe,
And slain, he told on Philip's plotting tribe.

Thus have I said, in my near circling soil,
How some have lived, and what has been their toil.
So Wallace, Bruce, and the free sturdy Switz
Drew inspiration from their mountain heights."

Tell why, one eve, I saw Blue Hill ablaze.

"The Land was Free just fifty years of days,
From my heart's burning crater shooting high
My flame, like Ætna's, burnished bright the sky;
Half-century freemen gleed in wild hurra;
They marched, they sang, they dined and told the War;
CRANE'S GUARDS marched here, with fife, and drum ajar;
Men piled on me with patriotic aim,
This summit tower, observe it here the same;
Doty-des, giant of those days, showed how
To lift the rocks and to fulfil the vow,
To place on high observed in lofty heaven
The proof that man's for Freedom's life was given.
So piled the Giants Ossa up above
On Pelion, then climbed and routed Jove—
Twice have the winds demolished wooden frames,
Oblivion sweeping off a thousand names
Of devotees, who, round my summit shrine,
Had cut their signs to show their faith divine.
Sharing *to-night* the ardor of my men
My crater's depths will shoot forth flame again."

Thanks for the speech so kindly spoke and true,
Centennial verse is sung, Blue Hill adieu!

By Ten Commands wrote out in Sinai's light,
By every promise beamed from Zion's height;
By Jove's bright bolts from high Olympus strewn,
By Nine Fair Maids on Helicon in tune;
By all the blest by Christ upon the Mount,
By all the saved on Calvary's account;
Abide as Pillar on the base our State,
Its ensign, beacon, hope, defender, mate,
Thou gavest her name, now give thy solid trait.

Ich bin der Knab vom Berge.

J. SPARE.